T0101476

THE ULTIMATE COLLECTION OF

BIBLE TRIVIA, PUZZLES, & FACTS

THE ULTIMATE COLLECTION OF

BIBLE TRIVIA, PUZZLES, & FACTS

THOMAS NELSON
Since 1798

The publisher sincerely appreciates all the whose jokes or information are used in this book. We have made every effort to quote the source for each piece of information used. If we have inadvertently left anyone out, please let us know.

Special thanks to Allen Peabody for his contribution to the humor in this book.

© 2000, 2011 by Thomas Nelson, a division of HarperCollins Christian Publishing, Inc.

Originally published as *Nelson's Amazing Bible Trivia, Book 2*, © 2000, 2011.

All rights reserved. No part of this book may be used or reproduced in any manner whatsoever without written permission of the publisher, except for brief quotations in critical reviews or articles.

Unless otherwise indicated, all Scripture quotations are from the New King James Version, © 1979, 1980, 1982 by Thomas Nelson.

ISBN 978-0-7852-3334-3

Printed in the United States of America

20 21 22 23 24 25 - LSC - 9 8 7 6 5 4 3 2 1

Table of Contents

1. An Angel Gets Its Wings 1
2. Bible Translations 23
3. Famous (and not-so-famous) Figures 59
4. I Believe in Miracles 85
5. Other Gods of Other Nations 111
6. Promises and Covenants 141
7. Say a Little Prayer for Me 163
8. Tell Me a Story 187
9. What Just Happened? 227
10. When? 265
11. Where in the World? 297
12. Women's Issues 319
13. When the Saints Go Marching In 349
14. Worship 381

Foreword

The Bible is full of fascinating information. We have discovered this as we have pored over the many questions and answers that make up this book! We take the Bible very seriously, as the inspired Word of God, and have worked very hard to ensure that this book is as accurate as possible. All references are to the New King James Version of the Bible; each question and answer has been examined to make sure the interpretation is accurate and treated with the utmost respect.

Be intrigued with the information you will discover! Not only do you hold in your hands a thousand questions about the Bible and other topics that relate to it, but you are given bits of information in the "How About That!" sections that will add to your knowledge about the Bible and the times in which it was written. We find these bits of information especially helpful, as they aid in placing the events of the Bible alongside those of secular history.

As you go through this book, you will no doubt be surprised, shocked, and even humored by the facts you will uncover. Laugh! Enjoy the Scripture that God has given us! Nurture your sense of humor. Remember: Solomon, renowned for his wisdom, said, "There is . . . a time to laugh!" (Ecclesiastes 3:4).

Finally, let us encourage one another with the knowledge and experience that studying the Bible develops in us. It is full of practical ideas for happiness and purpose in this life, as well as promises for the life eternal. Share it with friends and family. We hope to help add some curiosity to your study of the Bible through your enjoyment of *The Ultimate Collection of Bible Trivia, Puzzles, and Facts.*

Preface

I'm so glad you've picked up a copy of *The Ultimate Collection of Bible Trivia, Puzzles, and Facts*! I hope that this book will be helpful to you as you explore topics in the Bible and in Bible history. While some of the questions in this volume do not have their origin in biblical texts, they all relate to biblical topics in some manner and are all intended to be edifying in your study of the Bible.

While you personally enjoy the material you discover in this book, share it with your friends—this book is intended to be used by groups of people as well as individuals. Bring it to your Bible Study and use it as an ice breaker; use it in the car as a travel game; be creative! I'm sure you will find many ways to use this collection of information and humor, so enjoy!

Quick thanks and recognition: My roommates Katheryn Willy and Rebekah Dogg for their inspiration and unforgettable one-liners. To Gillian and Matthew, for their humor, help, and dedication. And, finally, my family—both old and new—I love you all very much!

—Kate Anderson, editor

An Angel Gets Its Wings

MULTIPLE CHOICE

1. **When he cloaked Himself as an angel, God appeared to whom by the spring on the way to Shur?**
   - **A.** Hagar
   - **B.** Abraham
   - **C.** a leprechaun
   - **D.** Sarah

ANSWERS p. 18

2. **Who appeared to Moses in the burning bush, according to Exodus 3:2?**
   - **A.** God
   - **B.** Yahweh
   - **C.** the Angel of the Lord
   - **D.** The Lord of Hosts

3. **How did the Angel of the Lord address Gideon?**
   - **A.** Gideon, the little wimp!
   - **B.** Gideon, man of God
   - **C.** Gideon, mighty warrior
   - **D.** mighty man of valor

4. **Why did the Angel of the Lord call out, "Abraham, Abraham!"**
   - **A.** so that he would turn and flee from danger
   - **B.** so that he would not sacrifice his son Isaac
   - **C.** because he was about to trip and fall into the animal's feeding trough, and he wanted to warn him

D. so that he would repent from his sin and turn to God

5. What animal did an angel appear to?

A. Balaam's donkey
B. Cleopatra's cat
C. Jonah's whale
D. Samson's lion

HOW ABOUT THAT!

Angels are most often depicted as women (Matt 22:30) yet when they appear in the Bible as humans they are described as men. (Gen 18, 19; Judg 13, Matt 28, Luke 24)

6. The Angel of the Lord declared God's covenant of protection with Israel void at Bochim because of Israel's sin in:

A. not obeying God
B. not sacrificing all the loot they recovered on their raids
C. the Watergate scandal
D. creating idols to worship instead of God

7. Where did the Angel of the Lord sit when he appeared to Gideon?

A. on Gideon's cloak, in the cool of the day
B. on a nettle
C. under the terebinth tree which belonged to Gideon's father
D. on the roof of Gideon's home

8. **What did the Angel of the Lord say to Manoah's wife?**

ANSWERS p. 18

A. she would give birth to Samuel
B. she would give birth to Isaiah
C. she would give birth to a submarine sandwich
D. she would give birth to Samson

FILL IN THE BLANKS

1. David saw an Angel of the Lord on the threshing floor _____ his people.

2. The Angel of the Lord commanded that David _____ _____ _____ on the _____ _____ of Ornan the Jebusite.

3. The Angel of the Lord provided _____ _____ _____ _____ _____ _____ _____ _____ _____ for Elijah to eat on his journey to Horeb.

4. The Angel of the Lord protected Elijah from _____ _____ _____ by sending fire from

Heaven on them, after Elijah prophesied Ahaziah's death.

5. Sennacherib's Assyrian army was defeated when the _____ ____ _____ _____ killed _____ _____ in their sleep.

6. The Angel of the Lord _____ ____ _____ to Zechariah, telling him to _____ _____ _____ _____ _____ _____.

7. In Zechariah's vision of the High Priest, _____ _____ _____ stood before the Angel of the Lord and _____ stood at his right hand to oppose him.

WORD BANK

a cake baked on coals and a jar of water

the high priest striking Satan

King Ahaziah's army threshing floor

proclaim the word of the Lord

built an altar explained a vision

MATCHING

ANSWERS p. 19

Quality of the Angel	Scripture Reference
1. Created Being	a. "Are they not all ministering spirits sent forth to minister for those who will inherit salvation?"
2. God's Servant	b. "Suddenly, a hand touched me, which made me tremble on my knees and on the palms of my hands."
3. Invisible	c. ". . . nor can they die anymore, for they are equal to the angels and are sons of God, being sons of the resurrection."
4. Limited Spatially	d. "Praise Him, all His angels . . . For He commanded and they were created."
5. Organized in Ranks	e. "For by him all things were created that are in heaven and that are on the earth, visible and invisible, whether thrones or dominions or principalities or powers."
6. Named	f. "Bless the Lord, you His angels, who excel in strength, who do His word, heeding the voice of His word."

MATCHING—cont'd

Quality of the Angel	Scripture Reference
7. Unmarried	g. "For in the resurrection they neither marry nor are given in marriage, but are like angels of God in heaven."
8. Spirits	h. "Now in the sixth month the angel Gabriel was sent by God to a city of Galilee named Nazareth . . ."
9. Undying	i. ". . . his face was like the appearance of lightning, his eyes like torches of fire, his arms and feet like burnished bronze in color, and the sound of his words like the voice of a multitude."
10. Blue, Smurfy	j. "La, la, la, la, la, la, la, la, la, la, la . . ."

TALL TALE

One day a very _____ angel was flying to _____ like she did every day. As she was going, she bumped into a _____

ADJECTIVE PLACE NOUN

that was not in a very _____ (ADJECTIVE)

mood. "_____ (APOLOGY)," she said to

the _____ (NOUN). "I didn't see you there!"

But the _____ (NOUN) simply looked at her like she

was a _____ (NOUN). The _____ (ADJECTIVE) an-

gel _____ (VERB (PAST TENSE)). The _____ (NOUN)

had made her very _____ (EMOTION). But

then, the _____ (NOUN) also began

to _____ (VERB (PAST TENSE))! The two be-

came _____ (ADJECTIVE) friends. From that day for-

ward, they went to _____ (PLACE) together every

day, and they lived _____ (EMOTION) ever after!

MATCHING

1. Hagar

2. Lot's Wife

a. Gabriel announced the birth of John the Baptist to him.

b. The Angel of the Lord announced an end to her barrenness and described the special nature of her son's ministry.

MATCHING—cont'd

3. Wife for Isaac	c. Angels led her and her family by the hand, away from their burning home.
4. Samson's Mother	d. Angels announced the birth of Jesus to them near Bethlehem.
5. Mary's betrothed	e. The Angel of the Lord gave helpful instructions, announced her future descendants, and offered comfort.
6. Women at the empty tomb	f. Gabriel told her that she would be the mother of the Messiah, even though she had never been with a man.
7. Elizabeth's husband	g. An angel calmed his fears of his wife's infidelity and announced her role in history to him.
8. Mary	h. An angel appeared to tell them that Jesus was alive.
9. Shepherds who came to see Mary and Jesus to the right woman.	i. An angel guided Abraham's servant

SHORT ANSWER

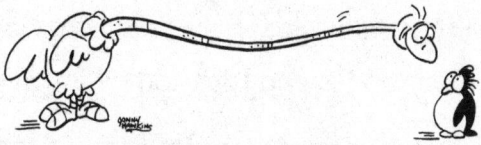

ANSWERS p. 20

1. What stood above the train of God's robe in Isaiah 6?

_____

2. What did the seraphim look like? _____

_____

3. What did the seraphim say to one another?

_____

_____

_____

4. Who said "Holy, holy, holy, Lord God Almighty, Who was and is and is to come" in Revelation?

_____

5. What is the name of the angel who saves George Bailey's life? _____

UNSCRAMBLE (the names for Satan)

1. Dabadon
2. Nolyopla
3. Ezebelubb
4. Liebla
5. Lived
6. Rangod
7. Neyem
8. Ficuler
9. Tanas
10. Petermt

ANSWERS p. 21

TRUE OR FALSE

1. Angels sleep.
2. Angels are called "sons of God."
3. Satan is called the god of this age.

4. The angels will bring peace among men on earth when Christ returns.

5. God, Himself, will separate the wicked from among the just at the end of the age.

6. The angels will gather the elect from the four winds, from the farthest part of earth to the farthest part of heaven.

7. An angel will bind Satan with a chain for one thousand years.

8. Satan is called the angel of the bottomless pit.

9. Angel hair pasta is made from actual angel hair.

10. The elder, not the angel, held the golden censer at the altar.

MULTIPLE CHOICE

1. **Angels appeared to Abraham in the form of:**
   - **A.** three men
   - **B.** white birds
   - **C.** W-4s
   - **D.** a multitude of women

2. **The angel who appeared as a "certain man" to Daniel wore what?**
   - **A.** a turban
   - **B.** sandals of sapphire
   - **C.** linen
   - **D.** a gold belt
   - **E.** adidas

ANSWERS p. 22

3. **The angel-men who wore shining garments appeared to whom at the tomb?**
   - **A.** Peter and Thomas
   - **B.** the women who had followed Jesus from Galilee
   - **C.** John and Peter
   - **D.** Peter, Paul, and Mary

4. **How do the angels minister in Psalm 104?**
   - **A.** with flames of fire
   - **B.** with a spirit of justice

Top Ten Ways the Angels Tried to Get Lot's Family to Leave Sodom and Gomorrah

10. Raised their taxes.
9. Threatened to take up an offering.
8. Left a trail of Reeses' Pieces.
7. Sent a steady stream of door-to-door salesmen to their house.
6. Convinced the neighbors to put giant satellite dishes in their front lawns.
5. Loaded his mailbox with junk mail.
4. "Rolled" his house every weekend.
3. Encouraged the neighbor kids to ride their bikes and skateboards through his well-kept yard.
2. They Sodom-ped on them.
1. Put his phone number on a telemarketing phone list.

C. with the Evangelism Explosion method
D. with a rod of discipline

5. In Psalm 68, God describes his angels as twenty-thousand what?
A. voices
B. stars
C. teeny-boppers
D. chariots

6. When did an angel rescue Paul?
A. when he had too much credit card debt
B. when he was in a storm on the sea
C. when he walked on water
D. when a crowd began to stone him

7. Angels do which of the following: (more than one answer)
A. announce events
B. quilt
C. attend church
D. carry messages
E. interpret visions
F. appear in dreams
G. investigate and punish sin

Q. How do we know angels don't use razors?
A. Because of the Christmas song: "Hark the hairy angel sings!"

H. watch over saints
I. marry

8. Which of the following people were guided by angels?
A. Hagar
B. Rebekah
C. Joseph
D. Cornelius
E. All of the above

ANSWERS TO: AN ANGEL GETS ITS WINGS

MULTIPLE CHOICE

#	ANSWER	REFERENCE
1.	a	Genesis 16:7–13
2.	c	Exodus 3:2
3.	d	Judges 6:12
4.	b	Genesis 22
5.	a	Numbers 22
6.	a	Judges 2
7.	c	Judges 6
8.	d	Judges 13

FILL IN THE BLANKS

#	ANSWER	REFERENCE
1.	striking	2 Samuel 24
2.	build an altar, threshing floor	1 Chronicles 21
3.	a cake baked on coals and a jar of water	1 Kings 19
4.	King Ahaziah's army	2 Kings 1
5.	angel of the Lord, 185,000 soldiers	2 Kings 19:35

#	ANSWER	REFERENCE
6.	explained a vision, proclaim the word of the Lord	Zechariah 1
7.	the high priest, Satan	Zechariah 3

MATCHING

#	ANSWER	REFERENCE
1.	d	Psalm 148:1–5
2.	f	Psalm 103:19–21
3.	e	Colossians 1:16
4.	b	Daniel 10:10–20
5.	i	Daniel 10
6.	h	Luke 1:26
7.	g	Matthew 22:30
8.	a	Hebrews 1:14
9.	c	Luke 20:36
10.	j	

MATCHING

#	ANSWER	REFERENCE
1.	e	Genesis 16:7–12
2.	c	Genesis 19
3.	i	Genesis 24:1–7

MATCHING—cont'd

#	ANSWER	REFERENCE
4.	b	Judges 13:1–24
5.	g	Matthew 1:20–25
6.	h	Matthew 28:2–6
7.	a	Luke 1:5–25
8.	f	Luke 1:26
9.	d	Luke 2:8–15

SHORT ANSWER

#	ANSWER	REFERENCE
1.	Seraphim	Isaiah 6
2.	Each one had six wings: two covered its face, two covered its feet, and with two it flew	Isaiah 6:2
3.	"Holy, holy, holy is the Lord of hosts; The whole earth is full of His glory!"	Isaiah 6:3
4.	The four living creatures, each having six wings, were full of eyes around and within.	Revelation 4:8
5.	Harold	

UNSCRAMBLE

#	ANSWER	REFERENCE
1.	Abaddon	Revelation 9:11
2.	Apollyon	Revelation 9:11
3.	Beelzebub	Matthew 12:24
4.	Belial	2 Corinthians 6:15
5.	Devil	John 8:44
6.	Dragon	Revelation 12:7
7.	Enemy	Matthew 13:39
8.	Lucifer	Isaiah 14:12–21
9.	Satan	Mark 1:12–13
10.	Tempter	1 Thessalonians 3:5

TRUE OR FALSE

#	ANSWER	REFERENCE
1.	False	Revelation 4:8
2.	True	Job 2:1
3.	True	2 Corinthians 4:4
4.	False	2 Thessalonians 1:7
5.	False	Matthew 13:49
6.	True	Mark 13:27
7.	True	Revelation 20:1–3
8.	True	Revelation 9:11
9.	False	
10.	False	Revelation 8:3

MULTIPLE CHOICE

#	ANSWER	REFERENCE
1.	a	Genesis 18
2.	c,d	Daniel 10
3.	b	Luke 24
4.	a	Psalm 104
5.	d	Psalm 68:17
6.	a,c,d,e,g,h	Luke 1, 1 Corinthians 11, Daniel 7–12, Genesis 18–19, Luke 12
7.	a,d,e,f,h	Genesis 16, 24; Judges 13, Matthew 1:20, Acts 10:3
8.	e	Acts 10:7

Q. What do angels and Martha Stewart have in common?

A. They are both heavenly hosts!

Bible Translations

MULTIPLE CHOICE

1. **The word "Bible" literally means:**
   - **A.** the books
   - **B.** the words of God
   - **C.** many words, small print
   - **D.** holy words

2. **Which group of people do NOT use the New Testament?**
   - **A.** Christians
   - **B.** Muslims
   - **C.** Jews
   - **D.** Saints

ANSWERS p. 39

3. **In the 18th and 19th centuries, and following, the divine inspiration of Scripture was:**
   - **A.** rejected
   - **B.** questioned
   - **C.** undoubtedly accepted
   - **D.** on vacation in the Caribbean

4. **Pope Leo XIII called the sacred writers:**
   - **A.** infallible geniuses
   - **b.** boy wonders
   - **C.** progenitors of God's will
   - **D.** instruments of the Holy Spirit

5. **Which word, meaning "a measuring rod, or a law," is the term used to describe the body of Scripture?**

A. canon
B. rifle
C. torah
D. septuagint

6. **Martin Luther suggested that which book be removed from the canon?**
   A. Leviticus
   B. Gone With the Wind
   C. The Gospel of Matthew
   D. The Epistle of James

7. **Which is NOT one of the three parts of the Hebrew Scriptures:**

A. Law
B. Poetry
C. Prophets
D. Writings

8. **Which of Josephus' rules for the Old Testament canon is incorrect:**
   A. the fixed number of books
   B. that they are sacred
   C. their divine origin
   D. that they were written between the time of Moses and Artaxerxes I

TRUE OR FALSE

1. Catholics and Protestants agree on which books should be included in the Bible.

2. The section of the Hebrew Old Testament called "Law" is also known as "The Pentatuch."

3. "The Prophets" is the section of the Bible that Protestants know as the books of Isaiah through Malachi.

4. In 200 B.C. major religious leaders gathered together and closed the Old Testament canon.

5. The B-I-B-L-E, that's the book for me!

ANSWERS p. 39

6. The apocrypha is the religious books not included in the canon of Scripture.

7. Most of the Old Testament was written in Hebrew, but parts were written in Aramaic and parts in Greek.

8. All of the New Testament was composed in Greek.

9. The first Old Testament book to be printed was Genesis in Bologna, A.D. 1477.

10. The Dead Sea Scrolls were discovered in caves near the ancient community of Qumran.

FILL IN THE BLANKS

1. The original manuscripts of the New Testament books are called _____.

2. God promised to _____ His Word.

3. _____ copied the manuscripts by _____.

4. Autographs were written in _____ Greek.

Top Ten Failed Bible Translations

10. Latin Vulgar
9. Revised Unauthorized Version
8. American Slandered Version
7. King Tut Version
6. New Irrational Version
5. New Umbilical Version
4. Fill-in-the-Blank Bible
3. Pig Latin Vulgate
2. The Bible According to Disney
1. Prehistoric Moments Bible

5. _____ _____ is the process of comparing different manuscripts to determine which version to follow.

6. _____ printed the first Greek New Testament in _____.

7. Erasmus' text was revised and improved and called the _____ _____.

8. The _____ _____ was compiled from manuscripts Erasmus found in _____, _____.

WORD BANK

modern	Textual criticism	digest
Reykjavik, Iceland	Fashion integration	
hand	folds	vernacular (everyday)
Erasmus, 1516	autographs	preserve
Elves	Nouveau Version	
Scribes	crayon	Textus Receptus
Raphael, 1731	Basel, Switzerland	

SHORT ANSWER

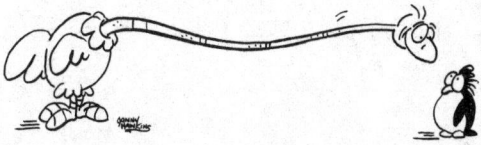

1. Who produced a very famous critical text of Scripture in A.D. 1882? _____

2. What method did Westcott and Hort use in producing their text? _____

_____

_____

_____

3. What contribution did J. J. Wettstein make to the printing of the New Testament? _____

_____

_____

4. The translation of the Hebrew Scriptures into Greek in the 3rd century B.C. is known as what?

_____

5. The legend surrounding the Septuagint says that this number of translators were sent from Jerusalem to Alexandria. _____

6. St. Jerome's translation of the Scriptures into Latin was called what? _____

7. The Vulgate was printed in A.D. 1455 by whom?

_____

8. The first Catholic Bible to be printed in the United States of America was printed in A.D. 1790 in what city? _____

HOW ABOUT THAT!

Martin Luther suggested that the book of James, among others, shouldn't be included in the Bible because of its emphasis on good works!

PUT THE FOLLOWING IN ORDER (from earliest to latest)

1. Tyndale Bible
2. New International Version
3. King James Version
4. Revised Version
5. Geneva Bible

ANSWERS p. 41

6. New King James Version
7. American Standard Version

MULTIPLE CHOICE

1. **Erasmus was a member of what church?**
   - **A.** Lutheran
   - **B.** First Baptist of Paducah
   - **C.** Catholic
   - **D.** Greek Orthodox

2. **Groups of manuscripts that are similar are called:**
   - **A.** text-types
   - **B.** common groups
   - **C.** look-alikes
   - **D.** manuscript groupings

ANSWERS p. 42

3. **Which of the text-types is the largest group?**
   - **A.** Alexandrian
   - **B.** Byzantine
   - **C.** Roman
   - **D.** Coptic

4. **Which text-types, older than Byzantine, came from Egypt?**
   - **A.** Alexandrian
   - **B.** Memphian
   - **C.** Nileian
   - **D.** Coptic

5. **Which text-type is called the Majority Text?**
   A. Alexandrian
   B. Roman
   C. the one that lots of people like to use
   D. Byzantine

6. **Which text-type were available to Erasmus?**
   A. Byzantine
   B. Roman
   C. Coptic
   D. boldfaced Times Roman

7. **Critical Texts usually include:**
   A. criticism from scholars
   B. bad attitudes

C. essays and maps
D. alternate wordings from other manuscripts

8. **Higher Criticism is when a scholar argues a text's:**
   A. height
   B. author and date
   C. location
   D. validity

MATCHING

Bible Version	Version It Is Based on or Translators
1. King James Version	a. Catholic Bible Association of America
2. Revised Authorized Version	b. American Standard Version
3. Revised Standard Version	c. Revised Standard Version
4. New English Bible	d. Bishop's Bible
5. Revised Version	e. King James Version
6. New American Bible	f. New King James Version
7. Jerusalem Bible	g. New York Bible Society

ANSWERS p. 42

MATCHING

Bible Version	Version It Is Based on or Translators
1. American Standard Version	h. La Bible de Jérusalem and Vulgate
2. New International Version	i. Revised Version
3. New Revised Standard Version	j. original languages only

FILL IN THE BLANKS

1. The _____ Bible was under censure during the Reformation and, therefore, was not _____.

2. _____ _____ translated the New Testament into German in 1522.

3. The Authorized Version, or _____ _____ _____, used much of _____'s translation without changing it.

4. In 1534, _____ was petitioned by the Canterbury Convocation to have the whole Bible translated into _____.

5. _____ _____, probably not knowing the _____ language, translated a Bible into English from German and dedicated it to the _____ of _____ in 1535.

ANSWERS p. 43

HOW ABOUT THAT!

The Printer's Bible, an early English translation, contains an ironic typo—"Printers have persecuted me without a cause." (Ps. 119:161)

6. The 1537 _____ _____ was the first Bible to receive the King's authorization.

7. Cromwell sponsored the printing of The _____ Bible in Paris in 1539.

8. The Geneva Bible became popular in England under the rule of _____ _____.

WORD BANK

Hebrew Queen Elizabeth I

Matthew Bible Martin Luther Wycliff

Great Henry VIII

King James Version English

printed Miles Coverdale King

England Tyndale

UNSCRAMBLE (the Bible translations)

1. Wne Tinarlonetian Sevrnio
2. Wen Rasujemle Libeb
3. Hutridoaze Risoven
4. Nigvil Bleib
5. Dogo Wesn Liebb
6. Nestiwretsm Sonevri fo het Lohy Pitresucrs
7. Viresde Danstrad Sivoner
8. Siprocue Temonsm Libeb
9. Lavugte Libbe
10. Dacoevrel's Elbib

ANSWERS p. 43

ANSWERS TO: BIBLE TRANSLATIONS

From http://www.pilgrimworks.com/trans.htm
The New Catholic Encyclopedia. Catholic UP: Washington, D.C., 1967.
The Oxford Dictionary of the Christian Church. Cross, F. L., ed.
Oxford UP: Oxford, 1997.

MULTIPLE CHOICE

#	ANSWER
1.	a
2.	c
3.	b
4.	d
5.	a
6.	d
7.	b
8.	d

TRUE OR FALSE

#	ANSWER
1.	False
2.	True

TRUE OR FALSE—cont'd

#	ANSWER
3.	False (also includes Joshua through Kings)
4.	False (There was never any meeting to close the Old Testament canon.)
5.	Up to you!
6.	True
7.	True
8.	True
9.	False (Psalms)
10.	True

FILL IN THE BLANKS

#	ANSWER
1.	autographs
2.	preserve
3.	Scribes, hand
4.	vernacular (or everyday)
5.	Textual criticism
6.	Erasmus, 1516
7.	Textus Receptus
8.	Textus Receptus, Basel, Switzerland

SHORT ANSWER

#	ANSWER
1.	Westcott and Hort
2.	verse-by-verse comparison
3.	capital letters
4.	the Septuagint
5.	72, thus the "septuagint"
6.	the Vulgate
7.	Johann Gutenberg
8.	Philadelphia

PUT THE FOLLOWING IN ORDER

#	ANSWER
1.	Tyndale Bible (1525)
2.	Geneva Bible (1557)
3.	King James Version (1611)
4.	Revised Version (1881)
5.	American Standard Version (1901)
6.	New International Version (1973)
7.	New King James Version (1982)

MULTIPLE CHOICE

#	ANSWER
1.	c
2.	a
3.	b
4.	d
5.	d
6.	a
7.	d
8.	b

MATCHING

#	ANSWER
1.	d
2.	f
3.	b
4.	j
5.	e
6.	a
7.	h
8.	i
9.	g
10.	c

FILL IN THE BLANKS

#	ANSWER
1.	Wycliff, printed
2.	Martin Luther
3.	King James Version, Tyndale
4.	Henry VIII, English
5.	Miles Coverdale, Hebrew, King, England
6.	Matthew Bible
7.	Great
8.	Queen Elizabeth I

UNSCRAMBLE

#	ANSWER
1.	New International Version
2.	New Jerusalem Bible
3.	Authorized Version
4.	Living Bible
5.	Good News Bible
6.	Westminster Version of the Holy Scriptures
7.	Revised Standard Version

UNSCRAMBLE—cont'd

#	ANSWER
8.	Precious Moments Bible
9.	Vulgate Bible
10.	Coverdale's Bible

Q. Why did St. Jerome buy a watch?

A. Because he was always translate!

TEXT AND TRANSLATIONS

ENGLISH VERSIONS

English readers have had access to many versions of the Bible in the past four centuries. This list gives the date, title, and translator of over 200 English versions of Scripture. It is based upon more extensive lists by John H. Skilton and A. S. Herbert. Where the translator's name is unknown, or where a group of translators contributed to a particular work, the version is identified by the publisher's name (shown in parentheses):

DATE	VERSION	TRANSLATOR/ PUBLISHER
1526	(The New Testament: untitled)	William Tyndale
1530	The Psalter of David in Englishe	George Joye
1530	(The Pentatuch: untitled)	William Tyndale
1531?	The Prophete Jonas	William Tyndale
1534	Jeremy the Prophete, translated into Englisshe	George Joye
1534	The New Testament	George Joye
1535	Biblia: The Byble	George Coverdale
1536	The Newe Testament yet once agayne corrected	William Tyndale
1537?	(The New Testament)	Miles Coverdale
1537	The Byble	(Richard Grafton and Edward Whitchurch)
1539	The Most Sacred Bible (Taverner's Bible)	Richard Taverner

DATE	VERSION	TRANSLATOR/ PUBLISHER
1539	The Byble in Englyshe (The Great Bible)	(Richard Grafton and Edward Whitchurch)
1539	The newe Testament of oure sauyour Jesu Christ	Miles Coverdale
1539	The Nevv Testament in Englysshe	Richard Taverner
1539	The new Testament in Englyshe	(Richard Grafton and Edward Whitchurch)
1540	The Byble in Englyshe	Miles Coverdale
1548?	Certayne Psalmes chose out of the Psalter	Thomas Starnhold
1549	The first tome or volume of the Paraphrase of Erasmus vpon The newe Testament	(Edward Whitchurch)
1557	The Nevve Testament of ovr Lord Jesus Christ	William Whitingham
1560	The Bible and Holy Scriptvres conteyned in the Olde and Newe Testament (The Geneva Bible)	William Wittingham
1562	The Whole Booke of Psalmes	Thomas Starnhold and I. Hopkins
1568	The holie Bible (The Bishops' Bible)	Matthew Parker
1582	The Nevv Testament of Iesvs Christ (Rheims New Testament)	Gregory Martin
1611	The Holy Bible (The King James Version)	(Robert Barker)
1612	The Book of Psalmes	Henry Ainsworth

DATE	VERSION	TRANSLATOR/ PUBLISHER
1657	The Dutch Annotations upon the whole Bible	Theodore Haak
1700	The Psalmes of David	C. Caryll
1726	A new version of all the Books of the New Testament	(J. Batly and S. Chandler)
1727	The books of Job, Psalms, proverbs, Eccleseastes, and the Song of Solomon	(J. Walthoe)
1731	The New Testament . . . Translated out of the Latin Vlugat by John Wiclif . . . about 1378	John Lewis
1741	A new version of St. Matthew's Gospel	Daniel Scott
1745	Mr. Whiston's Primitive New Testament	William Whiston
1761	Divers parts of the holy Scriptures	Mr. Mortimer
1764	All the books of the Old and New Testament	Anthony Purver
1764	The New Testament	Richard Wynne
1765	The Psalms of David	Christopher Smart
1765	The New Testament	Philip Doddridge
1768	A Liberal Translation of the New Testament	Edward Harwood
1770	The New Testament or New Covenant	John Worsley
1771	The Book of Job	Thomas Scott
1773	The Pentateuch of Moses and the Historical Books of the Old Testament	Julius Bate
1779	Isaiah	Robert Lowth

DATE	VERSION	TRANSLATOR/ PUBLISHER
1779	Essay towards a literal English version of the New Testament, in the Epistle of the Apostle Paul directed to the Ephesians	John Callander
1782	The Gospel of St. Matthew	Gilbert Wakefield
1784	Jeremiah and Lamentations	Benjamin Blayney
1787	The First (-Fifth) Book of Moses	David Levi
1787	The Apostle Paul's First and Second Epistles to the Thessalonians	James MacKnight
1789	A new English Translation of the Pentateuch	Isaac Delgado
1789	The Four gospels	George Campbell
1790	The Book of Psalms	Stephen Street
1791	The New Testament	Gilbert Wakefield
1795	The New Testament	Thomas Haweis
1796	Jonah	George Benjoin
1796	An Attempt toward revising our English translation of the Greek Scriptures	William Newcome
1797	The Holy Bible	Alexander Geddes
1799	A Revised Translation and Interpretation of the Sacred Scriptures	David Macrae
1805	The Book of Job	Joseph Stock
1807	The Gothic Gospel of Saint Matthew	Samuel Henshall
1808	The Holy Bible	Charles Thomson
1810	The Book of Job	Elizabeth Smith

DATE	VERSION	TRANSLATOR/ PUBLISHER
1811	Canticles: or Song of Solomon	John Fry
1812	The Book of Job	John Mason Good
1812	The New Testament	W. Williams
1816	The English Version of the Polyglott Bible	(Samuel Bagster)
1819	Lyra Davidis (Psalms)	John Fry
1822	The Epistles of Paul the Apostle	Thomas Belsham
1825	The Book of Job	George Hunt
1825	The Psalms	J. Parkhurst
1827	An Amended Version of the Book of Job	George R. Noyes
1827	Liber Ecclesiasticus, the Book of the Church	Luke Howard
1828	The Gospel of God's Anointed	Alexander Greaves
1831	The Book of Psalms	George R. Noyes
1833	A literal translation from the Hebrew of the twelve Minor Prophets	A. Pick
1833	A New and Corrected Version of the New Testament	Rodolphus Dickinson
1834	The Gospel according to Matthew	William J. Aislabie
1835	The Book of the Law from the Holy Bible (The Pentateuch)	Joseph Ablett
1837	A New Translation of the Hebrew Prophets	George R. Noyes
1837	The Gospel of John	William J. Aislabie
1843	The Gospel according to Saint Matthew, and part of the first chapter of the Gospel according to Saint Mark	Sir John Cheke

DATE	VERSION	TRANSLATOR/ PUBLISHER
1843	Horae aramaicae: comprising concise notices of the Aramean dialects in general and of the versions of the Holy Scripture extant in them: with a translation of Matthew	J. W. Etheridge
1846	The book of Psalms	John Jebb
1846	A New Translation of the Proverbs, Ecclesiastes and the Canticles	George R. Noyes
1846	The Four Gospels from the Peschito	J. W. Etheridge
1848	The New Testament	Jonathan Morgan
1848	St. Paul's Epistle to the Romans	Herman Heinfetter
1849	The Apostolic Acts and Epistles	J. W. Etheridge
1850	The Bible Revised	Francis Barham
1851	The New Testament	James Murdock
1851	The Epistle of Paul to the Romans	Joseph Turnbull
1851	The Epistles of Paul the apostle to the Hebrews	Herman Heinfetter
1854	The Epistles of Paul the Apostle	Joseph Turnbull
1855	The Book of Genesis	Henry E. J. Howard
1855	A Translation of the Gospels	Andrews Norton
1857	The Books of Exodus and Leviticus	Henry E. J. Howard
1858	The New Testament	Leicester A. Sawyer
1859	A Revised Translation of the New Testament	W. G. Cookesley

DATE	VERSION	TRANSLATOR/ PUBLISHER
1860	The Psalms	Lord Congleton
1861	Jewish School and Family Bible	A. Benisch
1861?	The New Testament . . . As Revised and Corrected by the Spirits	Leonard Thorn
1862	The New Testament	H. Highton
1863	The Holy Bible	Robert Young
1863	The Psalms	W. Kay
1863	The Book of Daniel	John Bellamy
1864	The Book of Job	J. M. Rodwell
1864	The Emphatic Diaglott	Benjamin Wilson
1867	The Minor Prophets	John Bellamy
1869	The Book of Job in metre	William Meikle
1869	The Book of Psalms	Charles Carter
1870	The New Testament	John Bowes
1871	The Book of Job	Francis Barham
1871	The Book of Psalms	Francis Barham and Edward Hare
1871	St. John's Epistles	Francis Barham
1871?	The Gospels, Acts, Epistles, and Book of Revelation	John Darby
1876	The Holy Bible	Julia E. Smith
1877	The New Testament	John Richter
1877	Revised English Bible	(Eyre and Spottiswoode)
1881	The New Testament: English Revised Version	(Kambridgel University Press)
1882?	St. Paul's Epistle to the Romans	Ferrar Fenton
1884	The Psalter . . . and certain Canticles	Richard Rolle

DATE	VERSION	TRANSLATOR/ PUBLISHER
1884	The Book of Psalms	T. K. Cheyne
1884	St. Paul's Epistles in Modern English	Ferrar Fenton
1885	The Old Testament Scriptures	Helen Spurrell
1885	The Holy Bible: Revised Version	(Oxford University Press)
1894	A Translation of the Four Gospels from the Syriac of the Sinaitic Palimpsest	Agnes S. Lewis
1897	The New Dispensation: The New Testament	Robert Weekes
1898	The Book of Job	Ferrar Fenton
1898	The Twentieth Century New Testament	(W. and J. Mackay and Co.)
1898	The Four Gospels	Seymour Spencer
1899	The Old and New Testament	(J. Clarke and Co.)
1900	St. Paul's Epistle to the Romans	W. G. Rutherford
1901	The Holy Bible: American Standard Version	(Thomas Nelson and Sons)
1901	The Five Books of Moses	Ferrar Fenton
1901	The Historical New Testament	James Moffatt
1902?	The Bible in Modern English	Ferrar Fenton
1903	The Book of Psalms	Kaufman Kohler
1903	The New Testament in Modern Speech	Richard Weymouth
1903	The Revelation	Henry Forster
1904	The New Testament	Adolphus S. Worrell
1906	St. John's Gospel, Epistles, and Revelation	Henry Forster
1908	Thessalonians and Corinthians	W. G. Rutherford

DATE	VERSION	TRANSLATOR/ PUBLISHER
1912	The Book of Ruth	R.H.J. Steuart
1913	The New Testament	James Moffatt
1914	The Poem of Job	Edward King
1916	The Wisdom of Ben-Sira (Ecclesiasticus)	W.O.E. Oesterley
1917	The Holy Scriptures according to the Masoretic text	(The Jewish Publication Society of America)
1918	The New Testament (The Shorter Bible)	Charles Foster Kent
1920?	Amos	Theodore H. Robinson
1921	The Old Testament (The Shorter Bible)	Charles Foster Kent
1921	Mark's Account of Jesus	T.W. Pym
1923	The New Testament. An American Translation	Edgar J. Goodspeed
1923	The Riverside New Testament	William G. Ballantine
1924	The Old Testament	James Moffatt
1924	Centenary Translation of the New Testament	Helen B. Montgomery
1925	Hebrews	F.H. Wales
1927	The Old Testament	J.M. Powis Smith, T.J. Meek, Alexander R. Gordon, Leroy Waterman
1927	St. Matthew's Gospel	(T. and T. Clark)
1928	The Psalms Complete	William W. Martin
1928	The Christian's Bible: New Testament	George LeFevre

DATE	VERSION	TRANSLATOR/ PUBLISHER
1933	The Four Gospels according to the Eastern Version	George M. Lamsa
1933	The Four Gospels	Charles C. Torrey
1936	The Song of Songs	W.O.E. Oesterley
1937	The Psalms and the Canticles of the Divine Office	George O'Neill
1937	The New Testament	Johannes Greber
1937	The New Testament	Charles B. Williams
1937	St. Paul from the Trenches	Gerald Cornish
1938	Job	George O'Neill
1938	The New Testament	Edgar L. Clementson
1939	Ecclesiasticus	A. D. Power
1944	The New Testament	Ronald A. Knox
1945	The Berkeley Version of the New Testament	Gerrit Verkuyl
1946	The Psalms . . . Also the Canticles of the Roman Breviary	(Benziger Bros.)
1946	The New Testament (Revised Standard Version)	(Thomas Nelson and Sons)
1947	The Psalms	Ronald A. Knox
1947	The New Testament	George Swann
1947	Letters to Young Churches: Epistles of the New Testament	J.B. Phillips
1949	The Old Testament	Ronald A. Knox
1950	The New Testament of Our Messiah and Saviour Yahshua	A.B. Traina
1950	New World Translation: New Testament	(Watchtower Bible and Tract Society)
1952	The Four Gospels	E.V. Rieu

DATE	VERSION	TRANSLATOR/ PUBLISHER
1952	The Holy Bible: Revised Standard Version	(Thomas Nelson and Sons)
1954	The New Testament	James A. Kliest and Joseph Lilly
1954	The Amplified Bible: Gospel of John	The Lockman Foundation
1955	The Authentic New Testament	Hugh J. Schonfield
1956	The Inspired Letters in Clearest English	Frank C. Laubach
1957	The Holy Bible from Ancient Eastern Manuscripts	George M. Lamsa
1958	The New Testament in Modern English	J.B. Phillips
1958	The Amplified Bible: New Testament	The Lockman Foundation
1959	The Holy Bible: The Berkeley Version in Modern English	(Zondervan Publishing Co.)
1960	The Holy Bible (New American Standard)	(Thomas Nelson and Sons)
1960	The New World Translation: Old Testament	(Watchtower Bible and Tract Society, Inc.)
1961	The New English Bible: New Testament	(Oxford University Press and Cambridge University Press)
1962	The Children's Version of the Holy Bible	J.P. Green
1962	Modern King James Version of the Holy Bible	(McGraw-Hill)
1962	Living Letters: The Paraphrased Epistles	Kenneth Taylor

DATE	VERSION	TRANSLATOR/ PUBLISHER
1962	The Amplified Bible: Old Testament Part II	The Lockman Foundation
1962	The New Jewish Version	Jewish Publication Society
1963	The New Testament in the Language of Today	William Beck
1963	The New American Standard Bible: New Testament	The Lockman Foundation
1964	The Amplified Bible: Old Testament Part I	The Lockman Foundation
1966	Good News for Modern Man: The New Testament	(American Bible Society)
1966	The Living Scriptures: A New Translation in the King James Tradition	(American Bible Society)
1966	The Jerusalem Bible	
1968	The Cotton Patch Version of Paul's Epistles	Clarence Jordan
1968	The New Testament of Our Master and Saviour	(Missionary Dispensary Bible Research)
1969	The New Testament: A New Translation	William Barclay
1969	Modern Language New Testament	(Zondervan Publishing Co.)
1969	The Cotton Patch Version of Luke and Acts	Clarence Jordan
1970	New American Bible	(St. Anthony Guild Press)
1970	New English Bible	(Oxford University Press and Cambridge University Press)

DATE	VERSION	TRANSLATOR/ PUBLISHER
1970	The Cotton Patch Version of Matthew and John	Clarence Jordan
1971	Letters from Paul	Boyce Black-Welder
1971	New American Standard Bible	The Lockman Foundation
1971	King James II Version of the Bible	(Associated Publishers and Authors)
1971	The Living Bible	(Tyndale House)
1972	The New Testament in Modern English, Revised Edition	J.B. Phillips
1973	The New International Version: New Testament	(Zondervan Bible Publishers)
1973	The Translator's New Testament	(The British and Foreign Bible Society)
1973	The Cotton Patch Version of Hebrews and the General Epistles	Clarence Jordan
1973	The Poetic Bible	Veo Gray
1976	Good News Bible	(American Bible Society)
1977	The Holy Bible in the Language of Today	William Beck
1978	The New International Version	(Zondervan Bible Publishers)
1979	The New King James Version: New Testament	(Thomas Nelson Publishers)
1982	The Holy Bible, New King James Version	(Thomas Nelson Publishers)
1986	The New Jerusalem Bible	
1989	New Revised Standard Bible	(Thomas Nelson Publishers and others)

DATE	VERSION	TRANSLATOR/ PUBLISHER
1989	Revised English Bible	(Oxford University Press and Cambridge University Press)
1991	Contemporary English Version, New Testament	(American Bible Society and Thomas Nelson Publishers)
1995	Contemporary English Version	(American Bible Society and Thomas Nelson Publishers)
1996	New Living Bible	(Tyndale Publishers)

Famous (and not-so-famous) Figures

MULTIPLE CHOICE

1. **Who hovered over the surface of the waters during Creation?**
   - **A.** arch-angels
   - **B.** cherubim and seraphim
   - **C.** the Spirit of God
   - **D.** Adam and Eve

ANSWERS p. 76

2. **Adam's name means:**
   - **A.** man
   - **B.** earth
   - **C.** first person
   - **D.** mankind's sorrow

HOW ABOUT THAT!

When King David was ruling Israel, the Chinese developed a textbook for Mathematics!

3. **Eve's name means:**
   - **A.** mother of all people
   - **B.** life-giver
   - **C.** lover of fruit
   - **D.** woman

4. **In which order were Adam, Eve, and the serpent cursed?**
   - **A.** Adam, Eve, Serpent
   - **B.** Eve, Adam, Serpent
   - **C.** Serpent, Eve, Adam
   - **D.** Kappa Alpha Order

MATCHING

1. Sarah	a. King Ahasuerus
2. Zipporah	b. Samuel
3. Gilbert	c. Moses
4. Rachel	d. Jacob
5. Potiphar's Wife	e. David
6. Esther	f. Abraham
7. Rebekah	g. Sullivan
8. Michal	h. Joseph
9. Hagar	i. Isaac
10. Hannah	j. Ishmael

ANSWERS p. 76

Q. What do John the Baptist and Winnie the Pooh have in common?

A. They both have the same middle name.

SHORT ANSWER

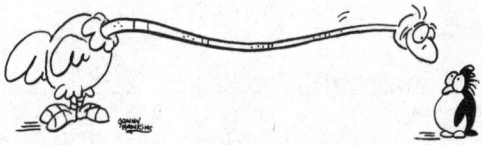

1. Of whom was it said, "This one shall give us rest from our work and from the toil of our hands arising from the ground which the Lord has cursed"?

   _____

2. Who said the following to whom? "Please let there be no strife between you and me, nor between my herdsmen and your herdsmen, for we are brothers."

   _____

3. List the ten miraculous deeds that the Lord performed through Moses and Aaron before Pharaoh.

   _____

   _____

   _____

4. Name Job's three friends. _____, _____, _____

ANSWERS p. 77

5. Define the following names of God.

   A. Abba _____

   B. Shaddai _____

   C. 'Elohim _____

D. 'Adonai _____

E. Yahweh _____

FILL IN THE FAMILY TREE

Hagar - - - - - - - - - - **1** - - - - - - - - - - Sarah

Ishmael

Isaac - - - - - - - - - - **2**

4 Rachel - - - Jacob - - - - Leah - - - Zilpah **3**

(Rachel's maid)

(Leah's maid)

Gad Asher

Dan Naphtali

5 **6**

7 Simeon Levi **8** Issachar Zebulun

TRUE OR FALSE

1. Miriam became leprous when she questioned God's speaking through Moses alone.

2. Sarah and Abraham had the same father.

3. Isaac loved Jacob and Rebekah loved Esau.

4. The phrase "Holiness to the Lord" appeared on a priest's turban.

ANSWERS p. 79

5. Chedorlaomer was a Pokemon.

6. The sun obeyed Joshua's command to stand still.

7. Samson's wife was a Moabite.

8. Saul was made King by his people in Israel.

9. Cyrus, the Persian King, declared that the captive Israelites should leave his land and build a temple for their Lord.

10. The Philistines sold the people of Judah and Jerusalem to the Greeks.

TALL TALE

One day a _____ (ADJECTIVE) man was walking down the street. He encountered a huge _____ (NOUN) and asked it how it was feeling. It said it was very _____ (EMOTION). So, the man wanted to help him. He took him to the nearby _____ (STORE NAME) to get some ice cream, because ice cream always makes you feel _____ (EMOTION). The man picked _____ (ICE CREAM FLAVOR), his favorite, but the _____ (NOUN) just got a _____ (BEVERAGE). This made the man _____ (SUPERLATIVE) _____ (EMOTION). He had wanted to help the _____ (NOUN) but it wouldn't budge. So, he realized, some _____ (NOUNS) just won't change no matter what you _____ (VERB). Before continuing on his way he _____ (VERB (PAST TENSE)) his ice cream and told the _____ (NOUN) he hoped he would _____ (COMMON PHRASE).

Moral of the story: _____ (MORAL).

WORD SEARCH

ANSWERS p. 80

Aaron	Eve	Lot	Sarah
Abel	Hagar	Melchizedek	Saul
Abraham	Haggai	Noah	Solomon
Adam	Jesus	Paul	Timothy
Andrew	John	Peter	Titus
Bathsheba	Joseph	Rachel	Xerxes
Cain	Levi	Rahab	

H	W	Q	E	R	T	Y	U	I	O	P	L	A	J	K	H	G	F	D	S
A	S	X	E	X	B	N	O	A	H	Z	T	A	M	N	P	E	T	E	R
G	M	J	K	B	E	E	J	K	N	M	C	R	U	T	A	P	I	L	A
G	L	C	A	I	N	R	K	J	C	D	W	O	X	Y	M	L	L	K	H
A	M	N	B	V	C	I	X	B	N	M	R	N	D	T	L	L	P	A	A
I	J	H	S	A	U	L	S	E	A	S	D	E	F	G	H	J	K	L	B
L	K	J	H	A	G	F	D	S	S	W	R	T	W	Y	U	I	O	P	M
M	N	B	A	B	R	A	H	A	M	V	E	S	A	Z	T	I	T	U	S
X	Y	U	J	E	B	A	T	H	S	H	E	B	A	J	K	L	B	M	C
L	J	H	P	L	B	A	H	G	U	I	K	L	N	J	E	S	U	S	G
X	E	R	X	A	N	M	U	T	Y	C	V	K	F	E	O	L	J	B	U
N	L	O	T	C	U	S	O	L	O	M	O	N	D	R	G	S	H	K	U
N	F	T	I	K	F	L	G	R	E	Y	M	Z	I	O	N	B	E	R	T
K	L	O	M	E	T	E	R	N	M	R	H	A	G	A	R	P	O	P	A
I	N	J	O	H	N	T	I	U	N	F	E	I	N	C	A	S	B	I	H
B	O	A	T	I	N	G	O	N	T	H	E	R	I	V	C	E	R	O	N
T	N	B	H	M	E	L	C	H	I	Z	E	D	E	K	H	E	W	V	K
L	O	P	Y	W	E	U	Y	T	R	B	D	H	K	I	E	X	V	Y	I
L	K	J	N	G	A	D	A	M	T	Y	C	V	U	I	L	E	V	I	Q
A	S	D	U	J	N	I	O	M	P	Q	U	Y	H	G	E	V	E	I	A

MULTIPLE CHOICE

1. **Jesus' birth to a virgin was predicted by which Old Testament Prophet?**
   - **A.** Daniel
   - **B.** Isaiah
   - **C.** Jeremiah
   - **D.** Nebuchadnezzar

2. **Jesus' birth in Bethlehem was predicted by which Old Testament prophet?**
   - **A.** Micah
   - **B.** Isaiah
   - **C.** 1-800-PSYCHIC hotline
   - **D.** Ezekiel

ANSWERS p. 81

3. **What did Tamar, Rahab, Ruth, and Mary have in common?**
   - **A.** They all auditioned for The Spice Girls—a volunteer organization of women who placed spices in the tombs of those who had died.
   - **B.** They are all in the genealogy of Jesus.
   - **C.** They all sang songs to God's glory.
   - **D.** They were all Jewish.

4. **What did Herod the tetrarch give to his wife's daughter for her birthday?**
   - **A.** silk from the Orient
   - **B.** a mustang convertible
   - **C.** the head of John the Baptist
   - **D.** the city of Tiberias

Top Ten Reasons God Created Eve

10. God worried that Adam would always be lost in the garden, because he hated to ask for directions.

9. God knew that Adam would one day need someone to straighten out his fig tie.

8. God knew that Adam would never buy a new fig leaf when his seat wore out and would therefore need Eve to get one for him.

7. God knew that Adam would never make a doctor's appointment for himself.

6. God knew that Adam would never remember which night was garbage night.

5. God knew that if the world was to be populated, men would never be able to handle childbearing.

4. As "Keeper of the Garden," Adam would never remember where he put his tools.

3. He had some extra parts left over.

2. As the Bible says, "It is not good for man to be alone!"

1. When God finished the creation of Adam, He stepped back, scratched His head and said, "I can do better than that."

5. **Which Jewish sect did not believe in the resurrection of the dead?**
   A. the Pharisees
   B. the Sadducees
   C. the Zealots
   D. the Wannabes

HOW ABOUT THAT!

Legend says that Luke, accepted writer of the gospel Luke and Acts, was an artist, and that in A.D. 590 Pope Gregory the Great used one of his paintings to lead a procession that stopped a plague!

FILL IN THE BLANKS

1. Who was the first martyr? _____

2. This queen's servant was converted by Philip on the road from Jerusalem to Gaza:

   _____

3. On Paul's first missionary journey he traveled to _____ and _____.

4. The book of Philemon is written about a _____ _____.

WORD BANK

John runaway slave Galatia and Cyprus

Candace, Queen of Ethiopia

Sodom & Gomorrah

MATCHING

1. Ethiopian Eunuch	a. the Road to Damascus
2. Jesus (after the resurrection)	b. the Road to Golgotha
3. Saul	c. the Road Again
4. Jesus and Simon a Cyrenian	d. the Road from Jerusalem to Gaza
5. Willie Nelson	e. the Road to Emmaus

TRUE OR FALSE

1. Titus went to work with the Corinthians.
2. Paul tells the Galatians how he confronted Andrew face to face in Antioch.
3. Paul speaks of the Whole Armor of God in Ephesians.

4. Elisha parted the Jordan River and crossed it after he saw Elijah taken up to heaven.

ANSWERS p. 82

5. Paul was married.

6. Onesimus was a runaway slave of the household of Philemon.

7. Hebrews was written by Paul.

8. Joseph worried about how Mary's pregnancy would look to other people.

9. John wrote, in Revelation, that the church of Ephesus lost their love for Jesus.

10. Jezebel appears in the book of Revelation and encourages believers at Smyrna to worship false gods.

CROSSWORD PUZZLE

QUESTIONS

ANSWERS p. 82

Across

1. The apostle formerly known as Saul
4. The seas struck during this trumpet's blast
6. Noah's and the title of a They Might Be Giants album
8. Has an affinity for fruit

9. The title of this book means "Law"
10. The Israelites' place of worship
13. She laughed when told she would have a child
14. The sound made by the "figurative" people of God
15. The last line of this 48-chapter book: "The Lord is there."
16. This angel had a flaming sword that "turned every direction" while he guarded the tree of life
17. This woman was saved from Jericho by placing a scarlet rope outside her window
19. This Old Testament figure asked to be a vegetarian
20. This treacherous man was the maternal grandfather of Joseph
21. This man blew trumpets and smashed pitchers to destroy an army
22. The governor of Judah (in Haggai 2:21)
24. What Mordecai and others put on their heads when they are desperate before God
27. Revelation's Seventh Seal
28. Adam, Eve, and _____ were cursed in the Fall
29. Pharaoh's _____ discovered Moses in a basket
30. Respect your _____.
31. The tax collecters were criticized for this
35. One name for Jesus
36. Abraham would have as many children as this
38. Isaac was saved by it
39. What Lazarus called Mary or Martha

40. This slave was a prince for a while
41. The first 5 books of the Bible
42. This king of Salem and famous High Priest blessed Abraham

Down:

2. city on the Lycus River in Phrygia, one of Asia's richest locations
3. This church was lukewarm
4. Jesus had this many disciples
5. The time of this event is unknown, but many have guessed
7. The tribe of priests
11. This king lost his mind and lived like an animal
12. Daniel and his friends survived this which made Nebuchadnezzar praise their God
18. Asa _____ Jehoshaphat
20. The greatest commandment
23. Paul used this genre of writing
25. Jacob's stealing of Esau's birthright showed _____ _____ for his family
26. This many seals were revealed to John
32. Mary's relationship to James and Jude
33. Hannah makes a _____ to God about the son she wishes to have
34. The two great lights and the stars were created on this day
37. If you play this, you are like David, glorifying God; if you are called this, you have broken the ninth commandment.

ANSWERS TO: FAMOUS (AND NOT-SO-FAMOUS) FIGURES

MULTIPLE CHOICE

#	ANSWER	REFERENCE
1.	c	Genesis 1:2
2.	a	
3.	b	
4.	c	Genesis 3:14–19

MATCHING

#	ANSWER	REFERENCE
1.	f	husband and wife—Genesis 17—18)
2.	c	husband and wife—Exodus 2:21
3.	g	musical duo of the late nineteenth century
4.	d	husband and wife—Genesis 29:28
5.	h	attempted seductress and victim of libel—Genesis 39

#	ANSWER	REFERENCE
6.	a	husband and wife—Ester 2:17
7.	i	husband and wife—Genesis 24:15ff
8.	e	husband and wife—1 Samuel 18:27
9.	j	mother and son—Genesis 16
10.	b	mother and son—1 Samuel 1)

SHORT ANSWER

#	ANSWER	REFERENCE
1.	Noah	Genesis 5:29
2.	Water in the Nile turned to blood	Exodus 7–11
	Frogs invade the land	
	Lice	
	Egyptian cattle die	
	Plague of boils	
	Plague of hail	
	Plague of locusts	
	Darkness over Egypt	
	Death of First Born	

SHORT ANSWER—cont'd

#	ANSWER	REFERENCE
4.	Eliphaz Bildad Zophar	Job 3:11
5.	Abba—Daddy Shaddai—Almighty; All-Powerful God 'Elohim—God; The Creator 'Adonai—Lord; The Master Yahweh—LORD; the most intimate name for God; the Israelites wrote it without the vowels: YHWHi	

FILL IN THE FAMILY TREE

#	ANSWER
1.	Abraham
2.	Rebekah
3.	Esau
4.	Bilhah
5.	Joseph
6.	Benjamin

#	ANSWER
7.	Reuben, the firstborn
8.	Judah—Genesis 36 and Matthew 1

TRUE OR FALSE

#	ANSWER	REFERENCE
1.	True	Numbers 12:2, 10
2.	True	Genesis 20:12
3.	False	Genesis 25:28
4.	True	Exodus 28:36–37
5.	False	Genesis 14:9
6.	True	Joshua 10:12–13
7.	False	Judges 14:2
8.	False	1 Samuel 11:15
9.	True	Ezra 1:1–2
10.	True	Joel 3:6

Q. Why did Elijah pour water over the steer on the altar?

A. To make gravy!

WORD SEARCH

H W Q E R T Y U I O P L A J K H G F D S
A S X E X B N O A H Z T A M N P E T E R
G M J K B E E J K N M C R U T A P I L A
G L C A I N R K J C D W O X Y M L L K H
A M N B V C I X B N M R N D T L L P A A
I J H S A U L S E A S D E F G H J K L B
L K J H A G F D S S W R T W Y U I O P M
M N B A B R A H A M V E S A Z T I T U S
X Y U J E B A T H S H E B A J K L B M C
L J H P L B A H G U I K L N J E S U S G
X E R X A N M U T Y C V K F E O L J B U
N L O T C U S O L O M O N D R G S H K U
N F T I K F L G R E Y M Z I O N B E R T
K L O M E T E R N M R H A G A R P O P A
I N J O H N T I U N F E I N C A S B I H
B O A T I N G O N T H E R I V C E R O N
T N B H M E L C H I Z E D E K H E W V K
L O P Y W E U Y T R B D H K I E X V Y I
L K J N G A D A M T Y C V U I L E V I Q
A S D U J N I O M P Q U Y H G E V E I A

Q. Who was the poorest man in the Bible?

A. Nickledemus!

MULTIPLE CHOICE

#	ANSWER	REFERENCE
1.	b	Isaiah 7:14
2.	a	Micah 5:2
3.	b	Matthew 1:3,5,16
4.	c	Matthew 14:3–11
5.	b	Matthew 22:23

FILL IN THE BLANKS

#	ANSWER	REFERENCE
1.	Stephen	Acts 7:59
2.	Candace, Queen of Ethopia	Acts 8:27
3.	Galatia and Cyprus	Acts 13–14
4.	runaway slave	Philemon 1

MATCHING

#	ANSWER	REFERENCE
1.	d	Acts 8:26
2.	e	Luke 24:13
3.	a	Acts 9:3
4.	b	Mark 15:21
5.	c	

TRUE OR FALSE

#	ANSWER	REFERENCE
1.	True	2 Corinthians 8:16–17
2.	False	Galatians 2:11
3.	True	Ephesians 6:10–19
4.	True	2 Kings 2:11–14
5.	Traditionally believed to be False. However, a close study of Philippians 4 raises doubts. In Phil 4:3 Paul addresses his "true companion," which is, in the greek, the word used for spouse—it literally means "yoke fellow."	
6.	True	Philemon 1
7.	The author of Hebrews in unknown.	
8.	True	Matthew 1
9.	True	Revelation 2:1–7
10.	False	Revelation 2:20–23

CROSSWORD PUZZLE

#	ANSWER

Across:

1. Apostle Paul
4. The Second

#	ANSWER
6.	Flood
8.	Eve
9.	Leviticus
10.	Tabernacle
13.	Sarah
14.	Baa
15.	Ezekiel
16.	Cherubim
17.	Rahab
19.	Daniel
20.	Laban
21.	Gideon
22.	Zerubbabel
24.	Ashes
27.	Trumpets
28.	Snake
29.	Daughter
30.	Elders
31.	Usury
35.	The Teacher
36.	Sands
38.	Ram
39.	Sis
40.	Mose

CROSSWORD PUZZLE—cont'd

#	ANSWER
41.	Pentatuch
42.	Melchizedek

Down:

#	ANSWER
2.	Seventy
3.	Laodicea
4.	Twelve
5.	Christs Return
7.	Levi
11.	Nebuchadnezzar
12.	Fiery Furnace
18.	Begat
20.	Love The Lord
23.	Letters
25.	His Disrespect
26.	Seven
32.	Their Mom
33.	Promise
34.	Fourth
37.	Lyre

I Believe in Miracles

SHORT ANSWER

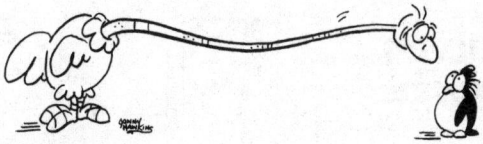

ANSWERS p. 101

1. What is the first miracle? _____

_____

2. How did Enoch die? _____

_____

3. Where did God enact the miracle of confusing language? _____

4. What did God do to Pharaoh's house when Sarah stayed there under the guise of Abraham's sister?

_____

_____

5. What miracle occurred when God changed Sarai's name to Sarah? _____

6. What did the angels do to the men who approached Lot's home? _____

7. How did God destroy Sodom? _____

_____

8. How did Lot's wife die? _____

MULTIPLE CHOICE

1. **What was Moses doing when God appeared to him in the burning bush?**
   - **A.** drawing water from his father-in-law's well
   - **B.** tending his father-in-law's sheep
   - **C.** tending his own sheep
   - **D.** commenting that his throat was on fire

HOW ABOUT THAT!

John, in his gospel, reports on seven miracles of Jesus. He also lists seven "I am" statements from Jesus. Both of these are used to prove that Jesus was God.

2. **Why was Moses' rod turned into a serpent?**
   - **A.** to impress Pharaoh
   - **B.** for extra protection from Pharaoh
   - **C.** so that the Egyptians would believe God had appeared to Moses
   - **D.** to shock the people into obedience

3. **What happened when Moses put his hand in his bosom?**

A. it turned leprous
B. it fell off
C. he passed out
D. it bled but no skin was broken

4. Which miracles did Moses and God talk about at the burning bush?
A. his rod turning into a serpent
B. parting the Red Sea
C. his hand becoming leprous
D. water from the Nile turning to blood

ANSWERS p. 101

5. When Moses and Aaron turned the water to blood how much water was affected?
A. just the water in the Nile
B. the water in the Nile, as well as ponds and tributaries
C. the water in the Nile, ponds, tributaries, buckets and pitchers
D. only the water at Pharaoh's feet

6. Pharaoh's magicians imitated which of the Lord's miraculous plagues on Egypt?
A. frogs
B. lice
C. darkness
D. bubonic

7. What did Aaron strike that became lice?
A. a nerve
B. stone
C. wood
D. dust

8. **Pharaoh's magicians gave credit to whom for the plague of lice?**
   A. Baal
   B. God
   C. Ra
   D. James Preston at 243 3rd Ave.

9. **Which of the following miracles occurred on the way to Sinai?**
   A. healing the bitter waters
   B. the miracle on 34th street
   C. quail provided by God
   D. victory over Amalek

10. **Which of the following were miracles of Elijah?**
    A. multiplies oil
    B. multiplies food
    C. restores rains
    D. purifies poison

11. **Which of the following were miracles of Elisha?**
    A. heals a spring
    B. purifies poison
    C. brings a drought
    D. destroys alter of Baal

12. **Which of the following miracles happened in Daniel?**
    A. Writing on the wall
    B. idol of Dagon falls on its face
    C. King Nebuchadnezzar's madness
    D. Israel delivered from captivity

Top Ten Plagues Not Inflicted on the Egyptians

10. Bad rap music

9. Ingrown toenails

8. Excessive navel lint

7. Bad hair days

6. Sluggish Internet providers

5. High insurance premiums

4. Overpopulation of Elvis impersonators

3. Allergies and leg cramps

2. Traffic delays due to construction

1. Grocery carts with one "bad" wheel

FILL IN THE BLANKS

1. God miraculously led his people by a _____ _____ _____ by day and a _____ _____ _____ by night.

2. The Lord said to Moses: "Lift up your _____, and stretch out your _____ over the _____ and divide it. And the children of Israel shall go on _____ _____ through the midst of the _____.

3. Moses cast a _____ into the waters at Marah to make them _____.

4. The Israelites complained that they would rather be in Egypt where they had _____.

5. The Israelites were to gather manna only _____ _____ _____ _____, except on the _____ day, when they were to gather _____.

6. In addition to manna, God also provided _____ for the Israelites to eat in the desert.

ANSWERS p. 102

7. _____ came out of the _____ when Moses struck it with his _____.

8. The Israelites defeated _____ as long as Moses _____ _____ _____ _____ _____ _____.

Q. Why was Peter unable to maintain his walk on the water?

A. He had a sinking feeling it wasn't going to last.

WORD BANK

tree quail water Amalek

rod wet ground sweet

food sixth rock

enough for one day

star rainbow dry ground

hand sea milk eighth

pillar of fire pillar of cloud

double Abraham

UNSCRAMBLE (the objects of miracles)

1. Erd Ase
2. Nideogs Elefec
3. Ticy fo Reijoch
4. Loi
5. Dojarn Evirr
6. Nilos Ned
7. Niew
8. Mostr

ANSWERS p. 103

SHORT ANSWER

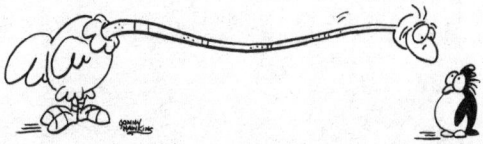

1. What happened to Aaron's rod that signified his family should be the priestly family? _____

_____

2. What did God send among the Israelites when they complained about their food and water? _____

_____

3. What did Balaam's donkey say to him when he saw the angel? _____

_____

4. How did Balaam react when the donkey spoke to him? _____

5. How did God separate the waters of the Jordan river? _____

_____

6. What did the Israelites do differently on their seventh trip around Jericho? _____

_____

_____

7. Who commanded the sun to stand still, and it did?

_____

_____

8. God chased and killed the Amorites with what force of nature? _____

_____

MULTIPLE CHOICE

1. **Jesus turned water into wine at:**
   - **A.** a wedding in Nazareth, his hometown
   - **B.** a wedding in Cana of Galilee
   - **C.** Jehosaphat's Bar and Grill
   - **D.** a wedding in Damascus

2. **Jesus healed the nobleman's son in:**
   - **A.** Cana of Galilee
   - **B.** Timbuktu
   - **C.** Damascus
   - **D.** Bethsaida

ANSWERS p. 104

3. **Jesus cast out an unclean spirit while preaching in a synagogue after it said to him:**
   - **A.** I am a legion, and I will destroy your work in the world.
   - **B.** I am a legion, and I know who you are—Son of Man.

C. I been noticin' you.
D. I know who You are—the Holy One of God!

4. Jesus healed Peter's mother of:
A. a demon
B. a tumor
C. a high fever
D. the stress Peter caused her

5. Whose boat was Jesus in when he miraculously caught a great number of fish?
A. Simon Peter's
B. John's
C. the Love Boat
D. Andrew's

6. **The man who was let in through the roof to see Jesus was:**
   A. dead
   B. paralyzed
   C. sick with a high fever
   D. a bad roofer

7. **When Jesus healed the man at the pool of Bethesda, he told:**
   A. the Pharisees, who sought to know where he lived
   B. the paparazzi, who sought to take a picture of him
   C. the Roman government, who sought to silence him
   D. the Jews, who sought to kill him

8. **The centurion believed that Jesus only had to do what for his servant to be healed?**
   A. say the word
   B. touch him
   C. the hokey-pokey
   D. send one of his disciples

TRUE OR FALSE

1. Jesus raised the son of the widow of Nain from the dead.

2. Jesus calmed the storm the same day that he told the parable of the sower.

3. The hemorrhaging woman was healed after she told Jesus she believed that he was the Christ.

4. The man whose daughter was healed was the ruler of the centurions.

5. Jesus healed two blind men who followed him and said, "Son of David, have mercy on us!"

6. Jesus fed the five thousand barley loaves and fish.

7. Jesus and the twelve disciples starred in the musical about their lives called *Godspell.*

8. After Jesus walked on the water, he got in the boat with the disciples and immediately the boat was at the place where they were going.

9. Jesus told the mother of the demon-possessed girl that it is not good to throw the children's food to the dogs.

10. To heal the deaf and dumb man, Jesus put His fingers in his ears, spat, touched his tongue, sighed and said, "Be opened," and he was healed.

Q. What time of day was Adam born?

A. Before Eve.

MATCHING

1. deaf and dumb man healed
2. man born blind healed
3. woman bound by Satan healed
4. man with dropsy healed
5. Lazarus raised from the dead
6. ten lepers healed
7. second catch of fish
8. graves opened at Calvary
9. Jesus' graveclothes were undisturbed
10. two disciples see the resurrected Jesus

a. Matthew
b. Mark
c. Luke
d. John

ANSWERS p. 105

ANSWERS TO: I BELIEVE IN MIRACLES

SHORT ANSWER

#	ANSWER	REFERENCE
1.	Creation	Genesis 1
2.	He didn't.	Genesis 5:19–24
3.	Tower of Babel	Genesis 11:1–9
4.	plagued them	Genesis 12:14–20
5.	fertility	Genesis 17:15–16
6.	struck them with blindness	Genesis 19:9–11
7.	with brimstone and fire	Genesis 19:24
8.	She turned into salt.	Genesis 19:26

MULTIPLE CHOICE

#	ANSWER	REFERENCE
1.	b	Exodus 3:1
2.	c	Exodus 4:5
3.	a	Exodus 4:6
4.	a,c,d	Exodus 4
5.	c	Exodus 7:19

MULTIPLE CHOICE—cont'd

#	ANSWER	REFERENCE
6.	a	Exodus 7–11
7.	d	Exodus 8:17
8.	b	Exodus 8:19
9.	a,c,d	Exodus 15, 16, 19
10.	b,c	1 Kings 17, 18
11.	a,b	2 Kings 4
12.	a,c	Daniel 4, 5

FILL IN THE BLANKS

#	ANSWER	REFERENCE
1.	pillar of cloud, pillar of fire	Exodus 12:21–22
2.	rod, hand, sea, dry ground, sea	Exodus 14:16
3.	tree, sweet	Exodus 15:26
4.	food	Exodus 16:3
5.	enough for one day, sixth, double	Exodus 16:4–5
6.	quail	Exodus 16:7–13
7.	Water, rock, rod	Exodus 17:6
8.	Amalek, held his hands in the air	Exodus 17:8–13

UNSCRAMBLE

#	ANSWER	REFERENCE
1.	Red Sea	Exodus 14
2.	Gideon's Fleece	Judges 6
3.	City of Jericho	Joshua 6–8
4.	Oil	2 Kings 4
5.	Jordan River	Joshua 3, 4
6.	Lions' Den	Daniel 6
7.	Wine	John 2
8.	Storm	Mark 4

SHORT ANSWER

#	ANSWER	REFERENCE
1.	this rod put forth buds and blossoms	Numbers 17
2.	fiery serpents	Numbers 21:4–9
3.	What have I done to you, that you have struck me these three times?	Numbers 22:28

SHORT ANSWER—cont'd

#	ANSWER	REFERENCE
4.	answered his question	Numbers 22:29
5.	the elders put their feet in and the water piled in a heap	Joshua 3–4
6.	shouted	Joshua 6
7.	Joshua	Joshua 10:12–13
8.	hailstorm	Joshua 10:10–11

MULTIPLE CHOICE

#	ANSWER	REFERENCE
1.	b	John 2
2.	a	John 4:46
3.	d	Luke 4:34
4.	c	Luke 4:38
5.	a	Luke 5
6.	b	Luke 5
7.	d	John 5
8.	a	Luke 7

TRUE OR FALSE

#	ANSWER	REFERENCE
1.	True	Luke 7
2.	True	Mark 4
3.	False	Matthew 9
4.	False	Luke 8
5.	True	Matthew 9
6.	True	John 6
7.	False	
8.	True	John 6:21
9.	True	Matthew 15:26
10.	True	Mark 7

MATCHING

#	ANSWER	REFERENCE
1.	b	Mark 7:31–37
2.	d	John 9
3.	c	Luke 13:10–17
4.	c	Luke 14:1–6
5.	d	John 11
6.	c	Luke 17:11–19

MATCHING—cont'd

#	ANSWER	REFERENCE
7.	d	John 21:1–14
8.	a	Matthew 27:52–53
9.	d	John 20:2–10
10.	c	Luke 24:13–35

THE MIRACLES OF JESUS CHRIST

1. Cleansing a Leper	Matthew 8:2; Mark 1:40; Luke 5:12
2. Healing a Centurion's Servant (of paralysis)	Matthew 8:5; Luke 7:1
3. Healing Peter's Mother-in-Law	Matthew 8:14; Mark 1:30; Luke 4:38
4. Healing the Sick at Evening	Matthew 8:16; Mark 1:32; Luke 4:40
5. Stilling the Storm	Mathew 8:23; Mark 4:35; Luke 8:22
6. Demons Entering a Herd of Swine	Mathew 8:28; Mark 5:1; Luke 8:26
7. Healing a Paralytic	Mathew 9:2; Mark 2:3; Luke 5:18
8. Raising the Ruler's Daughter	Mathew 9:18, 23; Mark 5:22, 35; Luke 8:40,49
9. Healing the Hemorrhaging Woman	Mathew 9:20; Mark 5:25; Luke 8:43
10. Healing Two Blind Men	Mathew 9:27
11. Curing a Demon-possessed, Mute Man	Mathew 9:32
12. Healing a Man's Withered Hand	Mathew 12:9; Mark 3:1; Luke 6:6
13. Curing a Demon-possessed, Blind and Mute Man	Mathew 12:22; Luke 11:14
14. Feeding the Five Thousand	Matthew 14:13; Mark 6:30; Luke 9:10; John 6:1

15. Walking on the Sea	Matthew 14:25; Mark 6:48; John 6:19
16. Healing the Gentile Woman's Daughter	Matthew 15:21; Mark 7:24
17. Feeding the Four Thousand	Matthew 15:32; Mark 8:1
18. Healing the Epileptic Boy	Matthew 17:14; Mark 9:17; Luke 9:38
19. Temple Tax in the Fish's Mouth	Matthew 17:24
20. Healing Two Blind Men	Matthew 20:30; Mark 10:46; Luke 18:35
21. Withering the Fig Tree	Matthew 21:18; Mark 11:12
22. Casting Out an Unclean Spirit	Mark 1:23; Luke 14:33
23. Healing a Deaf Mute	Mark 7:31
24. Healing a Blind Paralytic at Bethsaida	Mark 8:22
25. Escape from the Hostile Multitude	Luke 4:30
26. Draught of Fish	Luke 5:1
27. Raising of a Widow's Son at Nain	Luke 7:11
28. Healing the Infirm, Bent Woman	Luke 13:11
29. Healing a Man with Dropsy	Luke 14:1
30. Cleansing the Ten Lepers	Luke 17:11
31. Restoring a Servant's Ear	Luke 22:51
32. Turning Water into Wine	John 2:1
33. Healing the Nobleman's Son (of fever)	John 4:46

34. Healing an Infirm Man at Bethesda	John 5:1
35. Healing the Man Born Blind	John 9:1
36. Raising of Lazarus	John 11:43
37. Second Drought of Fish	John 21:1

Other Gods of Other Nations

CANAANITE GODS

MULTIPLE CHOICE

1. **Anat (or Anath) was a(n):**
   - **A.** Amorite warrior goddess
   - **B.** Hittite love goddess
   - **C.** Philistine goddess of wheat
   - **D.** Norwegian fish-boat captain

2. **Anat is a virgin and also:**
   - **A.** slave
   - **B.** queen
   - **C.** wet nurse
   - **D.** superstar

ANSWERS p. 131

3. **The first mention of Anat is around:**
   - **A.** 2000 A.D.—the new millenium!
   - **B.** 1780 B.C.
   - **C.** 1581 B.C.
   - **D.** 572 B.C.

4. **Asherah was the Canaanite mother of all the gods and represented:**
   - **A.** life giving and the primeval sea
   - **B.** familial relationships
   - **C.** perfect parenting
   - **D.** music and peace

5. **Asherah was the principal goddess of:**
   - **A.** the landlocked cities Ephesus and Alexandria
   - **B.** Damascus

C. the lost city of Atlantis
D. the coastal cities Tyre and Sidon

6. Canaanites considered Asherah to be a consort of:
A. Anat
B. the Israelite's God, El
C. the Wicked Witch of the West
D. Ninlil

7. Asherah's sons are:
A. in a singing group
B. Life, Death, and Humanity
C. Waves, Death, and Rabbim (the Many)
D. Water, Fire, and Sky

8. **The Phonecians created images of Asherah as a:**
   - **A.** pole
   - **B.** dog
   - **C.** elephant
   - **D.** cigarette

HOW ABOUT THAT!

Around the year 1 B.C., Druids living in Britain believed that they descended from a supreme being; the modern Wiccans found their beliefs on ancient Druidic philosophy.

TRUE OR FALSE

1. Astarte was the sister of Baal.
2. Astarte was the goddess of war, love, storms, the storehouse, and the evening star.
3. Solomon built a "high place" for Astarte.
4. Athar replaced Baal as high god of the Canaanites.
5. Baal was the father of Dagon.
6. The Greek god Zeus is derived from Baal.

ANSWERS p. 131

7. Dagon, god of the Philistines, fell on his face before the ark of the covenant.

8. The Philistine god Dagon and the Sumerian goddess Ninlil went to prom together.

9. The Canaanites thought of Elohim as a bull, thus the golden calf.

10. Horon was a major Canaanite god, the god of the underworld.

FILL IN THE BLANKS

1. El is the _____ God, also called _____.

2. Horon was the son of _____.

3. Sun was a Canaanite goddess called _____ torch and was the judge of the _____.

4. According to the Baal Cycle, Baal is _____ to explain the changing _____.

5. The story of the Baal Cycle mirrors that of the ancient writing _____ _____.

6. According to Judges 2, the Israelites abandoned _____ and served _____ and _____.

ANSWERS p. 132

7. But in 1 Samuel 7, the Israelites worshiped _____ instead of _____ and _____.

8. In Hosea 2, Yahweh tells Israel that they will call him, "_____ _____," and not "_____ _____."

Q. Why did the priests lose to Elijah in the "Battle of the Gods" on Mt. Carnel?

A. Their god couldn't "baal" them out!

WORD BANK

killed Astartes Yahweh

My husband Baal

Enuma Elish god Creator

Astarte god's seasons

My Baal

EGYPTIAN GODS

SHORT ANSWER

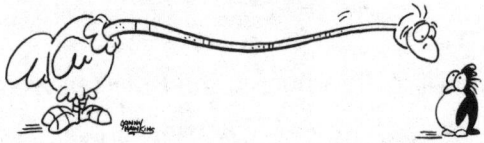

1. Which Egyptian diety was only viewed as an animal and never as a human with an animal head?

_____

2. Amen, the patron diety of the city of Thebes, is represented by what animals? _____

_____

3. Who was worshipped as the jackal god, inventor of embalming, and the son of Isis and Osiris?

_____

4. The Egyptians had a goddess who protected cats; what was her name? _____

5. Anuket was the dispenser of cool water and was represented in what form? _____

6. Who was depicted as a sun disk with rays, the only true diety during Amenhotep IV's reign? _____

7. The four sons of Horus protected parts of the body of whom? _____

8. What is the name of Amen's famous temple, the largest structure ever built by man? _____

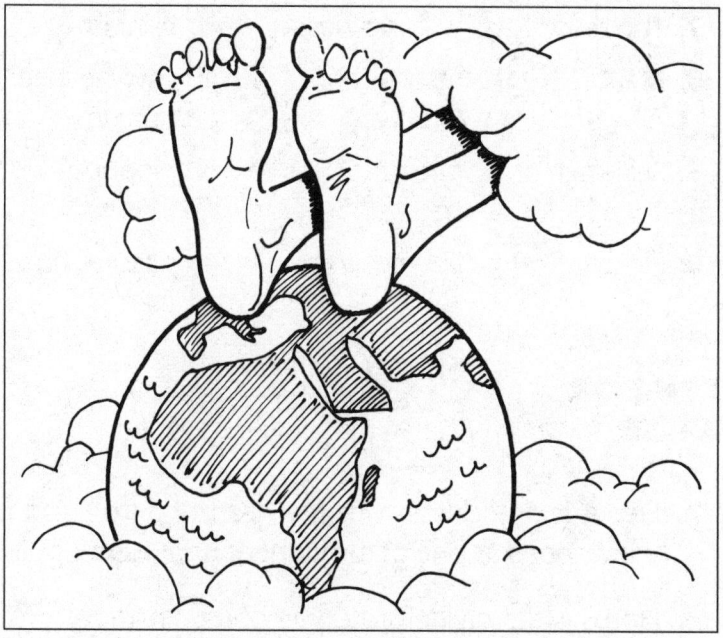

MATCHING

Goddess	Goddess of	Image
1. Edijo	a. love, beauty, joy	i. frog
2. Heqt	b. newborns, destiny	ii. human
3. Isis	c. fertility	iii. serpent
4. Thermuthis	d. fertility, women in labor	iv. lion-headed
5. Meskhenet	e. the Delta	v. serpent-headed
6. Hathor	f. justice	vi. serpent
7. Thoueris	g. war, sickness	vii. human
8. Maat	h. resurrection, fertility	viii. cow-headed human
9. Sekhmet	i. fate, fertility, harvest	ix. hippopotamus
10. Heket	j. life, healing	x. vulture, human

TRUE OR FALSE

1. Heqet is a goddess with the head of a frog and is worshipped as one of the eight gods at Hermopolis.

2. Horus is the divine prototype of the Pharaoh.

3. Imhotep was a historical figure who became diefied.

4. Isis was the mother of Osiris.

5. Isis was incapable of performing magic.

ANSWERS p. 134

6. The god Khepri is sybolized as a scarab beetle.

7. Maat was the daughter of Isis and Osiris.

8. Osiris ruled the world of men after Ra abandoned it to rule the sky.

9. Osiris is the god of the dead, resurrection into eternal life, ruler, protector, and judge of the deceased.

10. Ra, a hawk or hawk-headed man, was god of the sun in dynastic Egypt.

UNSCRAMBLE (names)

1. Nema
2. Patorharsec
3. Hempiot
4. Tama
5. Sisrio
6. Tisa
7. Busina
8. Joed
9. Queeth
10. Siis

ANSWERS p. 135

Top Ten Signs That You Need a New "God"

10. He often asks what you think he should do.

9. Instead of bowing in his presence, he prefers a gig.

8. When you tell him about your problems, he weeps uncontrollably.

7. When you pray, he usually responds, "Here's a quarter, find someone who care!"

6. He insists that you end your prayers with "ten four good buddy."

5. He's frequently overheard saying, "Oops!"

4. Not only is your god not omniscient, he can't even remember his own name!

3. He doesn't desire offerings and sacrifices, only shrubbery!

2. Forget parting seas, he can't even part his hair decently.

1. Your god has a life insurance policy.

BABYLONIAN GODS

MULTIPLE CHOICE

1. **Apsu, begetter of the skies and earth, could not:**
   - **A.** live within her creations
   - **B.** quell the noise of his children
   - **C.** get out of a speeding ticket
   - **D.** make his wife happy

2. **After her death, Tiamat's eyes became:**
   - **A.** jewels
   - **B.** sleepy
   - **C.** gates to heaven
   - **D.** sources for the Tigris and Euphrates rivers

3. **Lahmu and Lahamu wear:**
   - **A.** a triple sash
   - **B.** penguin suits
   - **C.** a golden necklace
   - **D.** rings of ruby

ANSWERS p. 135

4. **Anshar, father of Anu and son of Tiamat and Apsu—his name means:**
   - **A.** water and rain
   - **B.** really important guy
   - **C.** whole sky
   - **D.** earth and vegetation

5. **Anu's role was:**
   - **A.** father and king of the gods
   - **B.** to play with the animals

C. protector of Tiamat
D. guard of the underworld

6. **Aruru, the mother goddess, is responsible for:**
   A. velcro
   B. the creation of man
   C. the ethics of her children gods
   D. art among the mortals

7. **Mammetum made:**
   A. art
   B. death
   C. fate
   D. mmm good sandwiches

8. **Nammu is one of the:**
   A. gods of hate
   B. pure goddesses
   C. Jackson Five
   D. gods of destruction

SHORT ANSWER

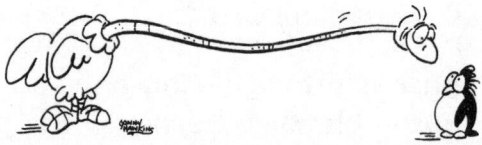

1. Ellil, leader of the pantheon, relinquished his throne to whom? _____

2. What is Ellil's sacred symbol? _____

3. Ea, Anshar's son, is the master of what crafts?

_____

4. Mummu, attendant to Ea and Apsu's vizier, is responsible for what? _____

5. What did Qingu give his army? _____

6. Sin, or Nannar, has a beard made of what?

_____

7. Ishtar is the goddess of what? _____

8. What human did Ishtar ask to be her husband—offering him gifts and status? _____

_____

MATCHING

1. Siduri	a. lawgiver, guarded by scorpion people
2. Nusku	b. Ellil's doorkeeper
3. Bel	c. god of fire
4. Kakka	d. the great wild cow
5. Zaltu	e. strife
6. Dumkina	f. barmaid
7. Ninsun	g. cleverest of gods
8. Marduk	h. Anshar and Anu's vizier
9. Shamash	i. central figure of Babylonian pantheon
10. Kalkal	j. mother of Bel and Marduk

ANSWERS p. 137

SUMERIAN GODS

TALL TALE

Once upon a time there was a _____ (ADJECTIVE) _____ (NOUN) that lived in a large _____ (NOUN) upon a hill. One day he decided to _____ (VERB) his dog. So they put on their _____ (NOUN) and _____ (VERB) the building. While they were gone, a _____ (ADJECTIVE) _____ (NOUN) _____ (ADVERB) broke into the house and _____ (VERB) all of man's _____ (NOUN), _____ (NOUN), and _____ (NOUN). When he returned with his _____ (NOUN), he found that all of his _____ (ADJECTIVE) things were missing. He _____ (ADVERB) called the _____ (NOUN) and _____ (VERB) them the _____ (NOUN). In _____ (NUMBER) minutes, the police _____ (VERB) the burglar and had _____ (ADVERB) _____ (VERB) him. The man was very _____ (ADJECTIVE).

FILL IN THE BLANKS

1. An's primary temple was in _____.

2. _____, An's female counterpart, was the progenitor of _____ of the _____.

3. Enlil was the _____ and _____ of the _____.

4. Enki was the god of _____, _____, and _____.

5. _____, daughter of Nanna, sought out as her lover, but he spurned her.

6. Nanna was the _____ _____, Sin.

ANSWERS p. 137

7. Utu goes to the _____ at the end of every day and decrees the _____ of the _____.

8. Ninlil was the intended bride of _____.

Q. What is the first commercial for soft drinks in the Bible?

A. The book of "Have-a-Coke!"

WORD BANK

Inanna, Gilgamesh

Erech most leader

gods moon god Enlil

underworld Ninhursag

air-god fertility fate

pantheon dead

TRUE OR FALSE

1. Nammu is the goddess of the watery abyss and Enki's sister.

2. Ningal begs Enlil to spare her city, Ur, from the flood.

3. Ereshkigal is the king of the underworld.

4. Nidaba was the goddess of wine.

5. Dumuzi was a shepherd when he was human.

6. Gilgamesh was probably the historical king of Erech.

7. Gilgamesh became a god.

8. Enkidu was Gilgamesh's brother.

9. Ningishzida was the god of dawn.

10. Neti was the chief gatekeeper.

ANSWERS p. 138

HOW ABOUT THAT!

Romans were generally not myth-makers; most of their myths were borrowed from other cultures.

WORD SEARCH

Liza (African)
Meher (Armenian)
Huitzilochtli (Aztec)
Lugh (Celt)
Ten Suns (Chinese)
Horus Bahdety (Egyptian)
Apollo (Greek and Roman)
Warusemn (Hittite)
Amaterasu (Japanese)
Tsohanoai (Navajo)
Freyr (Norse)
Radogast (Slavic)
Shamash (Sumerian)

A P O L L O K N A D C I P R U M Q J W T
L I N M N R E B J D H K N O D C U Y A M
L O H F I S G K H V D R K H F J V D R Y
K F C N H D T E N S U N S K N G R K U K
F R H B N H F K P T I A M A T E R A S U
P E M K F J F S T K P I E W A T R A E S
F R E Y R I P R X S J T U O C I O E M B
U W H I H C E J L M H X U T H E S O N S
M U E S T R O L E Y R A D I U S B X W J
Y T R A W S X L I Z A U I Q I N O P T Z
A S R E C S I U M V D H D G T U R X K I
P O T S H E R G D H O L X G Z E K O D R
Y H K D C W A H K I G F E T I U L R S B
Q A G I T L V Z P N A U S K L I V E B O
A N T C U A B O C Y S Z N D O G H I F J
R A S K W L N X M D T H O Q C I R P M S
H O R U S B A H D E T Y I S H A M A S H
Q I P Z A W M B K R V S J N T U X H G T
Y X V G V E U F F E D G W C L B F A L Q
L H E K I D M J R C T Q J F I K O Y Z P

ANSWERS TO: OTHER GODS OF OTHER NATIONS

CANAANITE GODS

MULTIPLE CHOICE

#	ANSWER
1.	a
2.	c
3.	b
4.	a
5.	d
6.	b
7.	c
8.	a

TRUE OR FALSE

#	ANSWER
1.	True
2.	True
3.	True

TRUE OR FALSE—cont'd

#	ANSWER
4.	False (failed to replace him and was made god of the underworld)
5.	False (his son)
6.	True
7.	True
8.	False
9.	True
10.	False (a minor god)

FILL IN THE BLANKS

#	ANSWER
1.	Creator, Elohim
2.	Astarte
3.	god's, gods
4.	killed, seasons
5.	Enuma Elish
6.	Yahweh, Baal, Astartes
7.	Yahweh, Baal, Astartes
8.	My husband, My Baal

EGYPTIAN GODS

SHORT ANSWER

#	ANSWER
1.	Apis, the bull
2.	goose and ram
3.	Anubis
4.	Bast
5.	gazelle with a feathered crown on her human head
6.	Aten
7.	Osiris
8.	Karnak

MATCHING

#	ANSWER	REFERENCE
1.	e	iii
2.	h	v
3.	j	ii
4.	i	vi
5.	b	x

MATCHING—cont'd

#	ANSWER	REFERENCE
6.	a	viii
7.	d	ix
8.	f	vii
9.	g	iv
10.	c	i

TRUE OR FALSE

#	ANSWER
1.	True
2.	True
3.	True
4.	False (wife and sister)
5.	False (She was a master magician.)
6.	True
7.	False (Ra)
8.	True
9.	True
10.	True

UNSCRAMBLE

#	ANSWER
1.	Amen
2.	Harpocrates
3.	Imhotep
4.	Maat
5.	Osiris
6.	Sati
7.	Anubis
8.	Edjo
9.	Heqetu
10.	Isis

BABYLONIAN GODS

MULTIPLE CHOICE

#	ANSWER
1.	b
2.	d
3.	a

MULTIPLE CHOICE—cont'd

#	ANSWER
4.	c
5.	a
6.	b
7.	c
8.	b

SHORT ANSWER

#	ANSWER
1.	Anu
2.	seven small circles representing the Pleiades
3.	writing, building, farming, and magic
4.	Tiamat's peace and quiet
5.	fire-quenching breath and paralyzing venom
6.	lapis lazuli
7.	love, procreation, and war
8.	Gilgamesh

MATCHING

#	ANSWER
1.	f
2.	c
3.	g
4.	h
5.	e
6.	j
7.	d
8.	i
9.	a
10.	b

SUMERIAN GODS

FILL IN THE BLANKS

#	ANSWER
1.	Erech
2.	Ninhursag, most, gods
3.	air-god, leader, pantheon

FILL IN THE BLANKS—cont'd

#	ANSWER
4.	water, creation, fertility
5.	Inanna, Gilgamesh
6.	moon god
7.	underworld, fate, dead
8.	Enlil

TRUE OR FALSE

#	ANSWER
1.	False (mother)
2.	True
3.	False (queen)
4.	False (writing)
5.	True
6.	True
7.	True
8.	False (servant)
9.	True
10.	True

WORD SEARCH

A	P	O	L	L	O	K	N	A	D	C	I	P	R	U	M	Q	J	W	T
L	I	N	M	N	R	E	B	J	D	H	K	N	O	D	C	U	Y	A	M
L	O	H	F	I	S	G	K	H	V	D	R	K	H	F	J	V	D	R	Y
K	F	C	N	H	D	T	E	N	S	U	N	S	K	N	G	R	K	U	K
F	R	H	B	N	H	F	K	P	T	I	A	M	A	T	E	R	A	S	U
P	E	M	K	F	J	F	S	T	K	P	I	E	W	A	T	R	A	E	S
F	R	E	Y	R	I	P	R	X	S	J	T	U	O	C	I	O	E	M	B
U	W	H	I	H	C	E	J	L	M	H	X	U	T	H	E	S	O	N	S
M	U	E	S	T	R	O	L	E	Y	R	A	D	I	U	S	B	X	W	J
Y	T	R	A	W	S	X	L	I	Z	A	U	I	Q	I	N	O	P	T	Z
A	S	R	E	C	S	I	U	M	V	D	H	D	G	T	U	R	X	K	I
P	O	T	S	H	E	R	G	D	H	O	L	X	G	Z	E	K	O	D	R
Y	H	K	D	C	W	A	H	K	I	G	F	E	T	I	U	L	R	S	B
Q	A	G	I	T	L	V	Z	P	N	A	U	S	K	L	I	V	E	B	O
A	N	T	C	U	A	B	O	C	Y	S	Z	N	D	O	G	H	I	F	J
R	A	S	K	W	L	N	X	M	D	T	H	O	Q	C	I	R	P	M	S
H	O	R	U	S	B	A	H	D	E	T	Y	I	S	H	A	M	A	S	H
Q	I	P	Z	A	W	M	B	K	R	V	S	J	N	T	U	X	H	G	T
Y	X	V	G	V	E	U	F	F	E	D	G	W	C	L	B	F	A	L	Q
L	H	E	K	I	D	M	J	R	C	T	Q	J	F	I	K	O	Y	Z	P

Promises and Covenants

TRUE OR FALSE

1. God's complete promise to Abraham was to make his descendents numerous and his nation great.
2. The Abrahamic covenant is the first promise in the Bible.
3. God promised to bless those who blessed Abraham.
4. God promised Noah that He would never again destroy the world.
5. God made His covenant with Moses on Mt. Sinai.
6. In the Davidic covenant, God told David that He would be a Father to him.
7. God promised that David's kingdom and house would endure before Him forever.
8. Nathan delivered God's promise to David.
9. God made his covenant directly with "Abraham."
10. The Mosaic covenant was intended to replace the Abrahamic covenant.

MULTIPLE CHOICE

1. **The Hebrew word for covenant is:**
   A. Qumran
   B. Mazel-Tov

C. Berit
D. Amen

2. **The three functions of the Mosaic covenant were to:**
   A. reveal God
   B. invent a perpetual motion machine
   C. reveal sin
   D. define God's expectations for man

HOW ABOUT THAT!

The New Covenant is first mentioned in the book of Jeremiah (31:31), which has more words than any other book in the Bible.

3. **Which covenants are found in Genesis?**
   A. Davidic
   B. Adamic
   C. Abrahamic
   D. New

4. **In the Abrahamic covenant, God first commands Abraham to:**
   A. sacrifice his son, Isaac
   B. get out of his country and away from his family and father's house

C. build an altar
D. start a pyramid scheme

5. **Abraham thought he had fulfilled God's covenant when:**
   A. he built an altar
   B. he left his home
   C. he made a hole in one on the 13th while playing with Lot
   D. Ishmael was born

6. **What did God do when Abraham asked how he knew the covenant would come to pass:**
   A. passed a smoking oven and burning torch between a sacrifice
   B. commanded him to be silent
   C. gave him a 3-pound kidney stone
   D. fulfilled the covenant

ANSWERS p. 157

7. **When did God change Abraham's name from Abram?**
   A. when He first appeared to him
   B. after he left his home at age 75
   C. when he was 99 years old
   D. after Isaac was born

8. **Who laughed when God promised Abraham and Sarah a child?**
   A. Abraham
   B. Sarah
   C. Isaac
   D. their pet hyena

FILL IN THE BLANKS

1. God saved Noah from the Flood because he was "_____ before God."

2. Noah and his family were in the ark for _____ days, but the rain only lasted _____ days.

3. God's promise to Noah was: "I will never again curse the _____ for _____'s sake, although the imagination of man's heart is

_____ from his _____;
nor will I again destroy every living thing as I
_____ _____."

4. God promises that seedtime and harvest, _____ and _____, _____ and _____, and day and night would last as long as the _____.

5. God blessed Noah and gave the _____ into his hand.

ANSWERS p. 158

6. God told Noah and his sons to _____ _____ and _____, and fill the earth.

7. The _____ is a sign of God's covenant with Noah to never destroy the earth _____ _____ again.

8. God's covenant with Noah had _____ requirements for mankind.

Q. Why did God promise not to destroy the earth by water again?

A. Because He knew his office would be flooded with complaints!

WORD BANK

cold cute multiply

smile by flood have done

40 heat cloud

animals evil by lightning

no 365 ground

youth summer earth

be fruitful rainbow

munchkins winter

MATCHING

1. Adam

2. Eve

3. Serpent

a. eat dust all the days of your life

b. sorrow will multiply

c. enmity between you and the woman

d. in toil you shall eat

e. in sweat you shall eat

f. your desire shall be for a mate

ANSWERS p. 159

3. Serpent—cont'd

g. you will return to dust

h. your clothes will be made from animal skins

i. you will be sent out of the garden

SHORT ANSWER

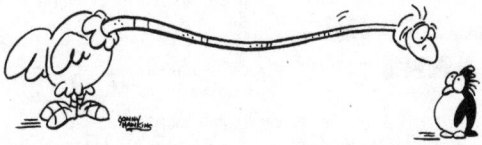

1. Who brought news of God's covenant with David to David? _____

2. What time of day did the word of the Lord come to Nathan? _____

3. What had David desired to do before he learned of the covenant? _____

4. What did God tell David He would do for the people of Israel? _____

5. Why was David not to build a Temple? _____

_____

6. What would be established forever? _____

_____

7. God promised to do what to Solomon, as well as establish his throne? _____

8. What was David's response to God's covenant?

_____

_____

_____

FILL IN THE BLANKS

1. God promises, in Amos 9, to _____ the damages to the tabernacle of David."

2. God shows his mercy on his people in Hosea 2 when he says, "I will _____ you to me in righteousness and justice, lovingkindness and mercy."

3. In Isaiah 1 God says, "If you are willing and _____, you shall eat the good of the land."

4. God tells Israel in Jeremiah 3, "I am _____ to you . . . I will bring you to Zion."

5. The coming of the Messiah is foretold in Micah 5, "But you, Bethlehem . . . out of you shall come forth to Me the One to be Ruler in _____."

6. God severely punished Israel in Ezekiel 5 because they "rebelled against my judgements by doing

more _____ than all the countries around her."

7. In Joel 2, God promises that He is "slow to anger and of great kindness, and _____ from doing harm."

All of these are examples of a _____ of God.

WORD BANK

forget	repair	obedient
relents	Israel	betroth
wickedness	married	

MULTIPLE CHOICE

1. **God promised Jacob that He would:**
   - **A.** give him invisibility superpowers
   - **B.** not leave until He fulfilled His Word
   - **C.** make him the ruler of many people
   - **D.** give him a place of honor among his people

2. **Joseph's promise of power over his brothers came to him in a(an):**

Top Ten Beatitudes That Didn't Make It

10. Blessed are the poor in wallet, for they shall be called mooches.

9. Blessed are those who mourn, for they shall receive Prozac.

8. Blessed are the geeks, for they shall make billions developing computer software.

7. Blessed are those who hunger and thirst, for they shall give McDonalds their business.

6. Blessed are those with rich relatives, for they shall inherit a fortune.

5. Blessed are the landscapers, for they shall see sod.

4. Blessed are the pure in heart, for they shall not need angioplasty.

3. Blessed are the pacemakers.

2. Blessed are those with Chex Mix, for they shall be the life of the party.

1. Blessed are you when people say all manner of evil against you falsely, for you shall be able to sue for slander.

A. dream about gold
B. instant message
C. dream about wheat
D. vision of famine

3. **God promised Moses what, which was the opposite of his fears:**
A. power
B. wealth
C. that his toses weren't roses
D. success

ANSWERS p. 160

4. **God promised to give Solomon which of his requests:**
A. wisdom
B. riches
C. honor
D. popularity with the ladies

5. **Naaman believed the prophet's promise of healing from what disease:**
A. blindness
B. strep throat
C. lame feet
D. leprosy

6. **Because Jehu did what was right in God's sight, God promised him:**
A. that his sons would sit on the throne for four generations
B. that he would rule a nation

C. a great stock option plan
D. wealth and prosperity

7. **Isaiah assured Hezekiah that his enemy would turn and go to his own land because:**
   A. he will be afraid of the size of Hezekiah's army
   B. his land will be attacked
   C. he will hear a rumor about his home
   D. he will get homesick for his momma

8. **God promised Josiah that he would not see**
   A. the death of his sons
   B. the calamity He would bring on this place
   C. the end of the reign of David
   D. the latest blockbuster movie

FILL IN THE BLANKS

1. The angel promised Mary she would _____ in her womb and bring forth a _____.

2. He also told her that Jesus would reign over the house of _____ forever.

3. After Peter declared Jesus was the Christ, Jesus said to him, "Blessed are you Simon _____, . . . on this _____ I will build my church."

4. Jesus promised the _____ that "there are some standing here who will not taste _____ until they see the kingdom of God _____ with power."

5. Jesus promised the disciples that they would receive the _____ _____ when He departed from them.

6. Jesus promised the thief on the cross that _____ they would meet in _____.

7. Zacharias was struck _____ when he questioned the promise of a _____.

8. The church elders (in 1 Peter 5) are promised a _____ of _____ that does not _____.

WORD BANK

Bar-Jonah, rock	today, Paradise
conceive, Son	crown, glory, fade
Jacob	disciples, death, present
mute, son	Holy Spirit

ANSWERS TO: PROMISES AND COVENANTS

TRUE OR FALSE

#	ANSWER	REFERENCE
1.	False	Genesis 12:2–7
2.	False	Genesis 3:14ff
3.	True	Genesis 12:2
4.	False	Genesis 9
5.	True	Exodus 19–20
6.	False	2 Samuel 7
7.	True	2 Samuel 7
8.	True	2 Samuel 7
9.	False	Genesis 12
10.	False	Galatians 3:15–18

MULTIPLE CHOICE

#	ANSWER	REFERENCE
1.	c	
2.	a,c,d	

MULTIPLE CHOICE—cont'd

#	ANSWER	REFERENCE
3.	b,c	Genesis 3, 15
4.	b	Genesis 12
5.	d	Genesis 15
6.	a	Genesis 15
7.	c	Genesis 17
8.	a,b	

FILL IN THE BLANKS

#	ANSWER	REFERENCE
1.	righteous	Genesis 7
2.	365, 40	Genesis 7–8
3.	ground, man's, evil, youth, have done	Genesis 8
4.	cold, heat, winter, summer, earth	Genesis 8
5.	animals	Genesis 9
6.	be fruitful, multiply	Genesis 9
7.	rainbow, by flood	Genesis 9
8.	no	Genesis 9

MATCHING

#	ANSWER	REFERENCE
1.	d,e,g,h,i	Genesis 2
2.	b,f,h,i	
3.	a,c	

SHORT ANSWER

#	ANSWER
1.	Nathan
2.	night
3.	build a Temple
4.	appoint a place for them
5.	God didn't desire one at the time—Solomon should build it.
6.	David's house and throne
7.	discipline him
8.	he praised Him and dedicated Israel to Him

FILL IN THE BLANKS

#	ANSWER
1.	repair
2.	betroth

FILL IN THE BLANKS—cont'd

#	ANSWER
3.	obedient
4.	married
5.	Israel
6.	wickedness
7.	relents

MULTIPLE CHOICE

#	ANSWER	REFERENCE
1.	b	Genesis 28:15
2.	c	Genesis 37:5
3.	d	Exodus 3:18
4.	a	1 Kings 3
5.	d	2 Kings 5
6.	a	2 Kings 10
7.	c	Isaiah 37
8.	b	2 Kings 22

FILL IN THE BLANKS

# ANSWER	REFERENCE
1. conceive, Son	Luke 1
2. Jacob	Luke 1
3. Bar-Jonah, rock	Matt 16
4. disciples, death, present	Mark 9
5. Holy Spirit	Acts 1:8
6. today, Paradise	Luke 23:43
7. mute, son	Luke 1:13
8. crown, glory, fade	1 Peter 5

Say a Little Prayer for Me

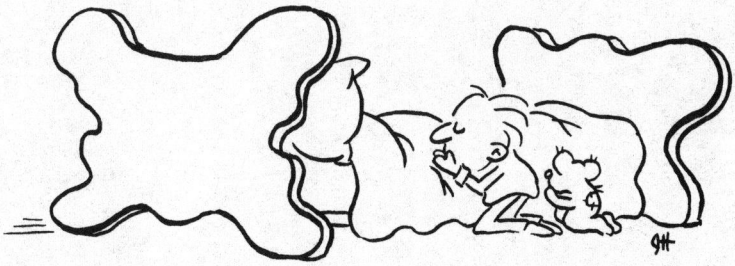

SHORT ANSWER

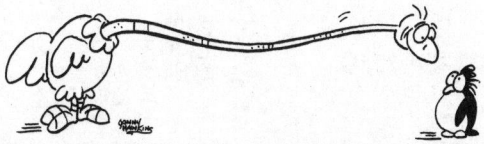

1. Paul prayed for what after being threatened by Jewish leaders in Acts? _____

2. How did the Lord first describe Saul of Tarsus to Ananias? _____

3. Paul commanded Simon the Sorcerer to pray for forgiveness from what? _____

4. Paul prayed and healed whom on the island of Malta? _____

5. The apostles named two men—Barsabbas and Matthias—and then prayed about what? _____

   _____

6. Paul prayed over Tabitha for what? _____

   _____

7. The apostles chose seven men to care for widows, and then prayed over them with what result?

   _____

8. What were Paul and Silas doing when their chains fell off in prison? _____

MATCHING

1. Abraham

2. David

3. Beniah

4. Gideon

5. Asa

6. Hezekiah

7. Dion Warwick

8. Amos

a. "Lord, it is nothing for you to help . . . do not let this man prevail against You!"

b. "May [the Lord] be with Solomon, and make his throne greater than the throne of my lord King David."

c. "If you will . . . give your maidservant a male child . . . no razor shall come upon his head."

d. "The moment I wake up, before I put on my makeup, I say a little prayer for you."

e. "Lord God of Abraham, Isaac, and Israel, let it be known this day that You are God in Israel and I am your servant."

f. "Oh, that Ishmael might live before You!"

g. "If You will save Israel by my hand as You have said—look . . ."

h. "O Lord, I pray, turn the counsel of Ahithophel into foolishness."

ANSWERS p. 178

9. Hannah — i. "Remember now, O Lord, I pray, how I have walked before You in truth and with a loyal heart, and have done what was good in your sight."

10. Elijah — j. "O Lord God, cease, I pray! Oh, that Jacob may stand, for he is small!"

HOW ABOUT THAT!

Many Roman Catholics pray on November 2 or All Souls' Day to hasten the transition of their dead loved ones from Purgatory to Heaven.

MULTIPLE CHOICE

1. **When Elisha prayed for the Lord to open the servant's eyes, his servant saw:**
   - **A.** hills full of horses and chariots of fire
   - **B.** towers crumbling
   - **C.** steam rising off the oceans
   - **D.** Elisha

2. **When he prayed before the Lord, Hezekiah spread out:**
   A. a fleece
   B. some "I Can't Believe It's Not Butter" on a roll
   C. a map
   D. a letter from King Sennacherib

3. **Whose request, "O that you would bless me and enlarge my territory," did God grant?**
   A. David's
   B. Jabez's
   C. Benji's
   D. Ahab's

ANSWERS p. 179

4. **When Jacob prayed because of his fear of Esau, he did what to his people for protection?**
   A. divided them into two groups, so one could run away
   B. gave them skins and told them to hide among the flocks
   C. gave them invisible suits, so that Esau wouldn't see them
   D. camped in the valley, so that they would see an army coming over the hills

5. **What was Jacob's attitude when he prayed for his sons?**
   A. proud
   B. sassy
   C. bereaved
   D. lonely

Top Ten Prayer Endings

10. Thank you and goodnight!

9. See ya!

8. Peace Out!

7. Hasta la vista, baby!

6. You have been a great audience, thank you!

5. I'm outta here!

4. Later, dude!

3. Until we meet again!

2. Watch your head on the way out!

1. Adios, amigo!

6. **Where did Jehoshaphat pray for Judah?**
   A. in Jerusalem, in the King's court
   B. in front of the new courtyard at the new Temple
   C. in the privacy of his tent
   D. he didn't

7. **How did the people of Bethel ask the Lord about fasting?**
   A. they offered sacrifices themselves
   B. they asked their leaders
   C. via e-mail
   D. they sent two leaders (and their men) to ask the priests and prophets

8. **What did Joshua pray after Israel defeated the Amorites?**
   A. that the Amonites wouldn't be too mad
   B. thanksgiving to God for his protection
   C. for the sun to stand still
   D. that the Amorites would be punished for their sins

TRUE OR FALSE

1. The Hebrew word "Amen" means "I now conclude."

2. The Egyptian plan for prayer was to manipulate the gods.

3. Lot prayed that his wife would become like "the salt of the earth."

4. When the Israelites worshipped the Golden Calf, Moses prayed, "Oh God, free me from service to these pagan people!"

5. Moses called on God to not respect the offering of a priest in a competition at the altar.

6. Naomi prayed that her daughters-in-law would remarry.

7. Elijah asked to be known as God's servant when he challenged the prophets of Baal.

8. After the pagan sailors threw Jonah overboard, they gloated in victory and cursed God.

9. Jesus prayed in the Garden of Gethsemane that God's will be done.

10. Isaiah, after being cleansed with coal, said to God, "Here am I, send me."

FILL IN THE BLANKS

1. After Elijah's victory over the pagan prophets of _____, he prayed, "It is enough! Now, Lord, take my _____, for I am no better than my _____."

2. Jonah _____ while in the belly of the fish, and then preached to _____, who he feared would _____.

3. When _____ confronted King David of his sin with _____, he confessed, "I have sinned against the _____."

4. Ezra confessed his sin _____, which led to a _____.

5. After Abraham's victory over the raiders who had captured his _____ Lot, _____ prayed a blessing over him.

6. Naomi's neighbors praised God for giving her a _____.

7. The Queen of Sheba praised _____ for making _____ king.

ANSWERS p. 180

8. Solomon praised God for his nation's _____.

9. Ezra praised God that a _____ ruler provided _____ to restore the _____.

10. Daniel asked God to _____ _____'s _____.

WORD BANK

grandson Baal Lord pagan
life nephew God Temple
reveal dream Melchizedek
Solomon peace fathers
Nathan publicly prayed
Bathsheba repent revival
funds Nebuchadnezzar's Ninevah

FILL IN THE BLANKS

1. David prays, in Psalm 16, "In your _____ is fullness of joy."

2. After the dedication of the house of David, he says (in Psalm 30), "I will give thanks to you _____."

3. The author of Psalm 38 tells God he will be in _____ over his sins.

4. During his exile in Judah, David wrote Psalm 63 saying, "My soul shall be _____."

5. In Psalm 3, David describes the protection of God as a _____.

6. Psalm 71 begs God to, "Be my strong _____."

WORD BANK

Forever	Refuge
Anguish	Shield
Satisfied	Presence

MATCHING

1. 'atar	a. to hear or listen to
2. palal	b. I pray.
3. paga'	c. to beg
4. shama'	d. to desire
5. sha'al	e. to answer
6. sha^{e}la	f. to intercede
7. sa'al	g. to pray
8. hanan	h. to beseech
9. 'ana	i. to request
10. na'	j. to entreat

ANSWERS p. 181

MULTIPLE CHOICE

1. **The rosary is a Roman Catholic prayer consisting of fifteen sets of ten:**
   - **A.** bicep curls
   - **B.** Hail Marys
   - **C.** rosarys
   - **D.** Mother Marys

2. **What book contains morning and evening prayers, as well as thirty-nine articles of religion:**
   - **A.** The English Book of Prayer
   - **B.** The Westminster Confession of Faith
   - **C.** The Complete Guide to WWJD?
   - **D.** Book of Common Prayer

3. **In Roman Catholic theology, prayers for the dead are for those people who are in:**
   - **A.** Purgatory
   - **B.** Hell
   - **C.** Heaven
   - **D.** Limbo

4. **Tibetan Buddhists use what when reciting mantras:**
   - **A.** prayer chains
   - **B.** prayer wheel
   - **C.** hula hoops
   - **D.** prayer books

5. **Which of the following statements is found in the Lord's prayer:**
   A. not my will but Thine be done
   B. give us this day our daily bread
   C. do unto us as we have done unto others
   D. I'm in the Lord's army

6. **What famous site in Jerusalem is the location of many Jewish prayers:**
   A. the temple of Jerusalem
   B. the market place
   C. the Wailing Wall
   D. the Church of the Sacred

ANSWERS p. 182

TRUE OR FALSE

1. Paul says that women should never pray aloud at church.

2. All early believers prayed in tongues.

3. Paul says we should pray "always."

4. Christians should pray for their rulers so that life will be quiet and peaceable in godliness and reverence.

5. The Holy Spirit is not involved with human prayers.

ANSWERS TO: SAY A LITTLE PRAYER FOR ME

SHORT ANSWER

#	ANSWER	REFERENCE
1.	boldness	Acts 4:23–31
2.	he is praying	Acts 9:11
3.	the thought in his heart	Acts 8:22
4.	Publius' father	Acts 28:8
5.	which one of the two should replace Judas	Acts 1:24
6.	that she would be raised from the dead	Acts 9:40
7.	the Word of God spread	Acts 6:7
8.	praying and singing hymns	Acts 16:25

MATCHING

#	ANSWER
1.	f
2.	h
3.	b
4.	g
5.	a
6.	i

#	ANSWER
7.	d
8.	j
9.	c
10.	e

MULTIPLE CHOICE

#	ANSWER	REFERENCE
1.	a	2 Kings 6:17
2.	d	2 Kings 19:14
3.	b	1 Chronicles 4:10
4.	a	Genesis 32:7–12
5.	c	Genesis 43:14
6.	b	2 Chronicles 20:5
7.	d	Zechariah 7:3
8.	c	Joshua 10:12

TRUE OR FALSE

#	ANSWER	REFERENCE
1.	False	"Let it be"
2.	True	
3.	False	
4.	False	Exodus 32:31

TRUE OR FALSE—cont'd

#	ANSWER	REFERENCE
5.	True	Numbers 16:15
6.	True	Ruth 1:9
7.	True	1 Kings 18
8.	False; They prayed.	Jonah 1:14
9.	True	
10.	True	Isaiah 6:8

FILL IN THE BLANKS

#	ANSWER	REFERENCE
1.	Baal, life, fathers	1 Kings 19:4
2.	prayed, Ninevah, repent	Jonah 4
3.	Nathan, Bathsheba, Lord	2 Samuel 12:13
4.	publicly, revival	Ezra 9
5.	nephew, Melchizedek	Genesis 14:20
6.	grandson	Ruth 4:14
7.	God, Solomon	1 Kings 10:9
8.	peace	1 Kings 8:56
9.	pagan, funds, Temple	Ezra 7:27
10.	reveal Nebuchadnezzar's dream	Daniel 2:20

FILL IN THE BLANKS

#	ANSWER
1.	Presence
2.	Forever
3.	Anguish
4.	Satisfied
5.	Shield
6.	Refuge

MATCHING

#	ANSWER
1.	j
2.	g
3.	f
4.	a
5.	c
6.	i
7.	d
8.	h
9.	e
10.	b

MULTIPLE CHOICE

#	ANSWER
1.	b
2.	d
3.	a
4.	b
5.	b
6.	c

TRUE OR FALSE

#	ANSWER	REFERENCE
1.	False	1 Corinthians 11
2.	False	1 Corinthians 14
3.	True	Ephesians 6:18
4.	True	1 Timothy 2
5.	False	Romans 8:26

As long as there are tests, there will always be prayer in school!

PRAYERS OF THE BIBLE

Abijah's army (for victory) ..... 2 Chronicles 13:14
Abraham (for a son) ..... Genesis 15:1–6
Abraham (for Ishmael) ..... Genesis 17:18–21
Abraham (for Sodom) ..... Genesis 18:20–32
Abraham (for Abimelech) ..... Genesis 20:17
Abraham's servant
(for guidance) ..... Genesis 24:12–52
Asa (for victory) ..... 2 Chronicles 14:11

Cain (for mercy) ..... Genesis 4:13–15
Centurion (for his servant) ..... Matthew 8:5–13
Christians (for Peter) ..... Acts 12:5–12
Christians (for kings in authority) ... 1 Timothy 2:1, 2
Corinthians (for Paul) ..... 2 Corinthians 1:9–11
Cornelius (for enlightenment) ..... Acts 10:1–33
Criminal (for salvation) ..... Luke 23:42, 43

Daniel (for the Jews) ..... Daniel 9:3–19
Daniel (for knowledge) ..... Daniel 2:17–23
David (for blessing) ..... 2 Samuel 7:18–29
David (for help) ..... 1 Samuel 23:10–13
David (for guidance) ..... 2 Samuel 2:1
David (for grace) ..... Psalm 25:16
David (for justice) ..... Psalm 9:17–20
Disciples (for boldness) ..... Acts 4:24–31

Elijah (for drought and rain) ..... James 5:17, 18
Elijah (for the raising to
life of the widow's son) ..... 1 Kings 17:20–23
Elijah (for triumph over Baal) ..... 1 Kings 18:36–38
Elijah (for death) ..... 1 Kings 19:4

Elisha (for blindness and sight)..... 2 Kings 6:17–23
Ezekiel (for undefilement) ..... Ezekiel 4:12–15
Ezra (for the sins of the people) ... Ezra 9:6–15

Gideon (for proof of his call)..... Judges 6:36–40

Habakkuk (for deliverance) ..... Habakkuk 3:1–19
Habakkuk (for justice) ..... Habakkuk 1:1–4
Hagar (for consolation) ..... Genesis 21:14–20
Hannah (for a son)..... 1 Samuel 1:10–17
Hezekiah (for deliverance)..... 2 Kings 19:15–19
Hezekiah (for health) ..... 2 Kings 20:1–11
Holy Spirit (for Christians) ..... Romans 8:26, 27

Isaac (for children) ..... Genesis 25:21, 24–26
Israelites (for deliverance) ..... Exodus 2:23–25
Exodus 3:7–10

Jabez (for prosperity)..... 1 Chronicles 4:10
Jacob (all night) ..... Genesis 32:24–30
Jacob (for deliverance for Esau) ... Genesis 32:9–12
Jehoahaz (for victory) ..... 2 Kings 13:1–5
Jehoshaphat (for protection) ..... 2 Chronicles 20:5–12, 27
Jehoshaphat (for victory) ..... 2 Chronicles 18:31
Jeremiah (for Judah) ..... Jeremiah 42:1–6
Jeremiah (for mercy) ..... Jeremiah 14:7–10
Jesus (Lord's Prayer) ..... Matthew 6:9–13
Jesus (praise for revelation
to babes)..... Matthew 11:25, 26
Jesus (at Lazarus' tomb) ..... John 11:41, 42
Jesus (for the Father's glory) ..... John 12:28
Jesus (for the Church) ..... John 17:1–26
Jesus (for deliverance) ..... Matthew 26:39, 42, 44
Matthew 27:46

Jesus (for forgiveness for others) ... Luke 23:34
Jesus (in submission) ..... Luke 23:46
Jews (for safe journey) ..... Ezra 8:21, 23
Jonah (for deliverance
from the fish) ..... Jonah 2:1–10
Joshua (for help and mercy) ..... Joshua 7:6–9

Leper (for healing) ..... Matthew 8:2, 3

Manasseh (for deliverance) ..... 2 Chronicles 33:12, 13
Manoah (for guidance) ..... Judges 13:8–15
Moses (for Pharaoh) ..... Exodus 8:9–13
Moses (for water) ..... Exodus 15:24, 25
Moses (for Israel) ..... Exodus 32:31–35
Moses (for Miriam) ..... Numbers 12:11–14
Moses (that he might see the
Promised Land) ..... Deuteronomy 3:23–25
Deuteronomy 34:1–4
Moses (for a successor) ..... Numbers 27:15–17

Nehemiah (for the Jews) ..... Nehemiah 1:4–11

Paul (for the healing of
Publius' father) ..... Acts 28:8
Paul (for the Ephesians) ..... Ephesians 3:14–21
Paul (for grace) ..... 2 Corinthians 12:8, 9
People of Judah (for a covenant) ... 2 Chronicles 15:12–15
Peter (for the raising of Dorcas) ... Acts 9:40
Priests (for blessing) ..... 2 Chronicles 30:27

Rebekah (for understanding) ..... Genesis 25:22, 23
Reubenites (for victory) ..... 1 Chronicles 5:18–20

Samson (for water) ..... Judges 15:18, 19
Samson (for strength) ..... Judges 16:29, 30

Samuel (for Israel) ..... 1 Samuel 7:5–12
Solomon (for wisdom) ..... 1 Kings 3:6–14

Tax collector (for mercy)..... Luke 18:13

Zechariah (for a son) ..... Luke 1:13

Tell Me a Story

FILL IN THE BLANKS

ANSWERS p. 206

1. The first parable told in the Gospel of Matthew is the parable of the _____.

2. In the Parable of the Sower, seed fell: _____ _____ _____, _____ _____ _____, _____ _____, and _____ _____ _____.

3. When Jesus explained the purpose of parables, he said, "Therefore I speak to them in parables because _____ they do not _____, and _____ they do not _____, nor do they understand."

4. The _____ asked Jesus to explain why he spoke in parables, and he told them they were _____.

5. In the Parable of the Wheat and Tares, Jesus said, "The kingdom of _____ is like a _____ who sowed _____ seed in his field; but while the man _____, his enemy came and sowed _____ among the wheat and went his way."

6. In the Parable of the Wheat and Tares the man _____ the tares and put the wheat in his _____.

7. The kingdom of heaven is like a _____ seed, which becomes a tree in which the birds of the air _____ in its branches.

8. The kingdom of heaven is like _____ which a woman took and hid in her _____ until it was all _____.

WORD BANK

barn seeing mustard citizens
unmerciful servant sunflower meal
basket heaven hear man
good leavened disciples slept
tares see sower by the wayside
leaven in stony places in the lake
burned hearing smell rotten
nest on good ground blessed
rocked tails

TRUE OR FALSE

1. Jesus did not explain the Parable of the Sower.
2. When Jesus spoke in parables, he spoke things that were kept secret from the foundation of the world.
3. Jesus explained the Parable of the Wheat and Tares to all the people who heard the parable.
4. In the Parable of the Hidden Treasure, the man sold all he had to buy a field.
5. In the Parable of the Pearl of Great Price, the man sold all he had to buy a pearl.
6. In the Parable of the Ugly Duckling, a huge man sings "fee fie fo fum" while two children eat a house made of candy.
7. In the Parable of the Dragnet, God Himself will separate the wicked from the just.
8. In telling the Parable of the Dragnet, Jesus asked the disciples if they understood "all these things."
9. According to the Gospel of Matthew, when Jesus finished telling the Parables of the Sower, Wheat and Tares, Mustard Seed, and Dragnet, he left for his home, Nazareth.
10. The point of the Parable of the Lost Sheep is the God cares about every one of his children.

MULTIPLE CHOICE

1. **In the Parable of the Lost Sheep, Jesus says that one should not despise children because:**
   - **A.** their angels always see the face of God
   - **B.** they possess the spirit that we should aim for
   - **C.** they're just so cute
   - **D.** their actions reflect the teachings of their parents

2. **How many sheep did the shepherd have?**
   - **A.** 1000
   - **B.** 100
   - **C.** 50
   - **D.** none, he lost them all

ANSWERS p. 207

3. **The Parable of the Unforgiving Servant was told in response to the question:**
   - **A.** "How do you catch a Pokémon?"
   - **B.** "Who will be the greatest in the kingdom of Heaven?"
   - **C.** "Who will sit at the right hand of Jesus in Heaven?"
   - **D.** "How often shall my brother sin against me, and I forgive him?"

4. **The Parable of the Unforgiving Servant ends with the servant:**

A. forgiven
B. standing next to a plane, saying, "This is the beginning of a beautiful friendship."
C. in jail and tortured
D. dead

5. **It is harder for a rich man to enter heaven than:**
   A. to find a needle in a haystack
   B. a camel to go through the eye of a needle
   C. a needle to go through the eye of a camel
   D. a sheep to find its way back to the fold

HOW ABOUT THAT!

The book of John contains no parables!

6. **In the Parable of the Workers in the Vineyard, the agreed wage was:**
   A. a denarius a day
   B. ten denarii a day
   C. ten denarii a week
   D. four pigs and one chicken per day

7. **Jesus ends the Parable of the Workers in the Vineyard by saying:**

A. All that are called are chosen.
B. I'm the king of the world.
C. Many are called but few are chosen.
D. The owner may choose those that it pleases him to choose.

8. The workers complained about
A. the heat
B. the people the owner chose
C. vacation days not rolling over
D. the amount of pay

SHORT ANSWER

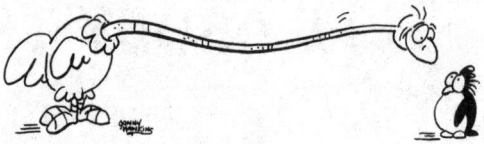

ANSWERS p. 208

1. Why did Jesus curse the fig tree? _____

_____

_____

2. What did Jesus say the disciples could do if they had faith? _____

3. In the Parable of the Two Sons, Jesus said that who believed before the priests and the elders believed?

_____

4. In the Parable of the Wicked Vinedressers, the vinedressers killed whom? _____

5. Who thought this parable was about themselves?

_____

6. What was their reaction to this parable? _____

_____

7. In the Parable of the Wedding Feast, who hosts the wedding? _____

8. What is the king's reaction to his servants' deaths?

_____

_____

UNSCRAMBLE (parables)

1. Wesor
2. Tusmard Dese
3. Tols Eshpe
4. Siwe dan Ofosilh Givirns
5. Dogo Masriatna
6. Lots Nico
7. Chir Lofo
8. Lantets
9. Degiwdn Eafst
10. Remnuifcul Verastn

ANSWERS p. 208

MATCHING

1. Lamp Under a Basket	a. Chief priests and Pharisees
2. The Marriage	b. Pharisees and Scribes
3. Patched Garment	c. Pharisees and Disciples of John
4. Leaven	d. Multitudes concerning John the Baptist
5. Pearl of Great Price	e. Disciples on the Mount of Olives
6. Wedding Garment	f. Disciples

7. Wise and Foolish Virgins — g. Multitude on the Seashore

8. Lost Coin

9. Persistent Widow

10. Children in the Marketplace

ANSWERS p. 209

FILL IN THE BLANKS

1. The Parable of the Fig Tree illustrates how to recognize the _____ _____.

2. The kingdom of heaven will be like ten _____, five of whom are _____ and five are _____.

3. The Parable of the Wise and Foolish Virgins is an illustration of what will happen at _____ _____ _____ _____ _____ _____.

4. In the Parable of the _____, the master congratulated the _____ and _____ servants by saying, "Enter into the joy of your lord."

5. The unprofitable servant in the Parable of the _____ will be cast into the _____ _____ where there will be _____ and _____ of teeth.

6. The first parable in the book of Mark is the Parable of the _____, and it comes right after Jesus' _____ and _____ send for him.

7. Jesus said, "Is a _____ to be put under a _____ or under a bed? . . . There is nothing _____ which will not be _____."

8. The Parable of the Growing Seed says, "The _____ of God is as if a man should scatter _____ on the ground, and should sleep by _____ and rise by _____, and the _____ should sprout and grow."

Q. Why did the disciples run out of the field where Jesus was speaking?

A. Because they saw a pair of bulls!

WORD BANK

day victors hidden

new earth virgins kingdom

night brothers outer darkness

basket cents seed end times

talents lamp revealed weekend

mother singing sower sister

wise hidden

the coming of the Son of Man

foolish faithful good brother

MULTIPLE CHOICE

1. **Jesus did not speak to the people without what, according to Mark 4:34?**
   A. moral lessons
   B. parables
   C. his lawyer present
   D. his disciples listening and learning

2. **Jesus, in speaking to the disciples about salt, said everyone will be seasoned with:**

Top Ten Parables That Didn't Make It

10. Parable of the Lost Man (who wouldn't ask for directions)

9. Parable of the Drunkards in the Vineyard

8. Parable of the Sewer

7. Parable of the Good Politician

6. Parable of the Lost Jeep

5. Parable of the Talent Agent

4. Parable of the Hairnet

3. Parable of the Fig Newton

2. Parable of the Unmerciful Detergent

1. Parable of the Mustard Stain

A. trials
B. paprika
C. fire
D. salt

3. When people brought their little children to see Jesus, the disciples:
A. rebuked them
B. welcomed them
C. taught them
D. babysat them

ANSWERS p. 210

4. Who gave more to the church than all the rich who had contributed to the treasury?
A. the Pharisees
B. Zacchaeus
C. Bill Gates
D. the widow with two mites

5. The fig tree's leaves will wither away unlike:
A. a bad facelift
B. the Word of God
C. the Temple of God
D. the heavens and the earth

6. What topic was Jesus discussing with the teachers in the temple as a child when his parents found him there?
A. we don't know
B. interpretations of the Torah

C. whether or not they would change his grade from a B+ to an A
D. the laws regarding the Jewish diet

7. **The story in which the wise man built his house upon the rock is a lesson about:**
A. carpentry
B. faith
C. hypocrisy
D. predestination

8. **In the Parable of the Sower, the seed that was sown by the wayside:**
A. was choked by rocks
B. was eaten by hairy cows
C. grew into a giant beanstalk
D. was trampled and eaten by birds

TALL TALE

One day a _____ (NOUN) was walking with two friends when it approached a _____ (NOUN) in the road. It _____ (VERB (PAST TENSE)), "Oh my stars! I've just seen a _____ (ADJECTIVE) _____ (NOUN)! I can't believe it!" So, the two friends and it _____ (VERB (PAST TENSE)) the _____ (NOUN) and put it in their _____ (ROOM OF HOUSE). They invited all their other friends over to _____ (VERB) it. But one friend did not think this exploitation was right—he confronted his friends. "You should not be so _____ (CHARACTER TRAIT) with this that you have discovered!" His friends listened to him and _____ (VERB). So, they let the _____ (NOUN) go back to where it had come from, and they all lived in _____ (IDEAL SETTING) from then on.

Moral: _____ (MORAL).

SHORT ANSWER

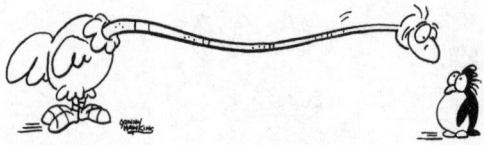

1. When Jesus explained the Parable of the Sower, what happened to those whose seed was sown onto the rocks? _____

2. Those whose seed fell on the good ground dc what? _____

3. What is the point of the Parable of the Revealed Light? _____

4. The Parable of the Good Samaritan only appears in which gospel? _____

5. Who tested Jesus, that he told the Parable of the Good Samaritan? _____

6. What did the Samaritan do for the wounded man?

   _____

7. Why did Jesus tell the Parable of the Rich Fool?

   _____

   _____

8. What happened to the Rich Fool when he had an overabundance of crops that he desired to keep for the years to come? _____

WORD SEARCH

Lost Coin
Sower
Dragnet
Pearl of Great Price
Wheat and Tares
Talents
Great Supper
Two Sons
Minas
Good Samaritan
Fig Tree

ANSWERS p. 212

K E L U P G D U J B X E I Y P V X E I M
N V G K O A L P V A E P L N C S D L E N
W H E A T A N D T A R E S O B W I O H C
L F E X B J Y O L M V A S G Y K N S B D
I G R L M B O Y T V H R E K P T D T Z U
E T U E R W Q M P A J L I V T K D C F B
P T W O S O N S C O W O N E C I R O T V
U A B Y H G F K L D O F Z Q P M I I N T
W L H S I G T A E F I G T R E E H N O P
U E S O E D G B I I R R L Y S A K N A D
T N H D E E R B Y B N E B I E E T Q H Z
A T N Y N V S H H G E A L T L I Y G R E
E S B R E D R A G N E T K V A I H K F I
L N E G T S C M H A E P R G B D E L S T
F B R R I I E A N N D R J O M I N A S B
N E O A X N F D O Y R I H D A U R N O I
M V O E N R H S U I T C Y S D C O A W R
N A G R E A T S U P P E R J B O B H E N
A M N O S E E S C N R G E U T S S T R O
G O O D S A M A R I T A N C V I O E N T

ANSWERS TO: TELL ME A STORY

FILL IN THE BLANKS

#	ANSWER	REFERENCE
1.	Sower	Matthew 13
2.	by the wayside, in stony places, among thorns, on good ground	Matthew 13
3.	seeing, see, hearing, hear	Matthew 13
4.	disciples, blessed	Matthew 13
5.	heaven, man, good, slept, tares	Matthew 13
6.	burned, barn	Matthew 13
7.	mustard, nest	Matthew 13
8.	leaven, meal, leavened	Matthew 13

TRUE OR FALSE

#	ANSWER	REFERENCE
1.	False—did not explain	Matthew 13
2.	True	Matthew 13, Psalm 78:2
3.	False—only the disciples	Matthew 13

#	ANSWER	REFERENCE
4.	True	Matthew 13
5.	True	Matthew 13
6.	False	
7.	False—angels will	Matthew 13
8.	True	Matthew 13
9.	True	Matthew 13
10.	True	Matthew 18

MULTIPLE CHOICE

#	ANSWER	REFERENCE
1.	a	Matthew 18
2.	b	Matthew 18
3.	d	Matthew 18
4.	c	Matthew 18
5.	b	Matthew 19
6.	a	Matthew 20
7.	c	Matthew 20
8.	d	Matthew 20

SHORT ANSWER

#	ANSWER	REFERENCE
1.	because nothing grew on it but leaves	Matthew 21
2.	move a mountain into the sea	Matthew 21
3.	tax collectors and harlots	Matthew 21
4.	servants and the owner's son	Matthew 21
5.	chief priests and Pharisees	Matthew 21
6.	wanted to lay hands on him but feared the people	Matthew 21
7.	the King, for his son	Matthew 22
8.	sent out armies and burned the cities, then invited strangers	Matthew 2

UNSCRAMBLE

#	ANSWER
1.	Sower
2.	Mustard Seed
3.	Lost Sheep

#	ANSWER
4.	Wise and Foolish Virgins
5.	Good Samaritan
6.	Lost Coin
7.	Rich Fool
8.	Talents
9.	Wedding Feast
10.	Unmerciful Servant

MATCHING

#	ANSWER	REFERENCE
1.	f	Mark 4
2.	c	Matthew 9
3.	c	Mark 2
4.	g	Matthew 13
5.	f	Matthew 13
6.	a	Matthew 22
7.	e	Matthew 25
8.	b	Luke 15
9.	f	Luke 18
10.	d	Luke 7

FILL IN THE BLANKS

#	ANSWER	REFERENCE
1.	the end times	Matthew 24
2.	virgins, wise, foolish	Matthew 25
3.	the coming of the Son of Man	Matthew 25
4.	talents, good, faithful	Matthew 25
5.	talents, outer darkness, weeping, gnashing	Matthew 25
6.	sower, mother, brothers	Mark 4
7.	lamp, basket, hidden, revealed	Mark 4
8.	kingdom, seed, night, day, seed	Mark 4

MULTIPLE CHOICE

#	ANSWER	REFERENCE
1.	b	Mark 4:34
2.	c	Mark 9:50
3.	a	Mark 10:13
4.	d	Mark 12:43
5.	b	Mark 13:28
6.	a	Luke 2

#	ANSWER	REFERENCE
7.	c	Luke 6
8.	d	Luke 8

SHORT ANSWER

#	ANSWER	REFERENCE
1.	have no root and in time of temptation fall away	Luke 8
2.	keep it and bear fruit with patience	Luke 8
3.	to whoever has, more will be given; whoever does not have, even what he seems to have will be taken away	Luke 8
4.	Luke	Luke 10
5.	a lawyer	Luke 10
6.	bandaged his wounds, poured oil and wine on him, had him taken care of at an inn	Luke 10
7.	a man in the crowd demanded that Jesus tell his brother to divide an inheritance between the two	Luke 12
8.	he died	Luke 12

WORD SEARCH

K E L U P G D U J B X E I Y P V X E I M
N V G K O A L P V A E P L N C S D L E N
W H E A T A N D T A R E S O B W I O H C
L F E X B J Y O L M V A S G Y K N S B D
I G R L M B O Y T V H R E K P T D T Z U
E T U E R W Q M P A J L I V T K D C F B
P T W O S O N S C O W O N E C I R O T V
U A B Y H G F K L D O F Z Q P M I I N T
W L H S I G T A E F I G T R E E H N O P
U E S O E D G B I I R R L Y S A K N A D
T N H D E E R B Y B N E B I E E T Q H Z
A T N Y N V S H H G E A L T L I Y G R E
E S B R E D R A G N E T K V A I H K F I
L N E G T S C M H A E P R G B D E L S T
F B R R I I E A N N D R J O M I N A S B
N E O A X N F D O Y R I H D A U R N O I
M V O E N R H S U I T C Y S D C O A W R
N A G R E A T S U P P E R J B O B H E N
A M N O S E E S C N R G E U T S S T R O
G O O D S A M A R I T A N C V I O E N T

TEACHINGS AND ILLUSTRATIONS OF CHRIST

Abiding in Christ ..... John 15:4–10
Ability ..... Matthew 25:14,15
Ablution ..... Matthew 6:17,18
Abode ..... John 14:23
Abraham ..... John 8:37, 56
Abstinence ..... Luke 21:34
Abundant life ..... John 10:10
Access to God ..... John 10:7,9
Accountability ..... Luke 12:47,48
Accusation, false ..... Matthew 5:11
Adultery ..... Matthew 5:27,28
Adversity ..... Luke 24:46
Affliction ..... Matthew 24:7–12
Agreement ..... Matthew 18:19
Altar ..... Matthew 23:18,19
Ambition ..... Luke 22:25–30
Angels ..... Matthew 13:39,41
Anger ..... Matthew 5:22
Anxiety ..... Luke 12:22–31
Apostasy ..... Matthew 13:18–22
Luke 8:13
Apostles ..... Luke 11:49
Appearance ..... Matthew 6:16
Appearance, outward ..... Matthew 23:27, 28
Authority ..... Matthew 21:24
Luke 10:19
Avarice ..... Luke 12:16–21

Backsliding ..... Luke 9:62
Baptism ..... Acts 1:5
Matthew 28:19
Beatitudes ..... Matthew 5:3–11
Beelzebub ..... Matthew 10:25

Begging ..... Luke 16:3
Beneficence ..... Matthew 5:42
Betrayal ..... Matthew 26:21
Bigotry ..... Luke 18:9–14
Birds ..... Matthew 8:20
Blasphemy ..... Matthew 12:31, 32
Blessings ..... Matthew 5:3–11
Blind guides ..... Matthew 15:14
Borrowing ..... Matthew 5:42
Bread of Life ..... John 6:32–35
Brothers ..... Matthew 23:8
Builders ..... Luke 6:47–49
Matthew 7:24
Burdens ..... Luke 11:46
Burial ..... Matthew 8:22

Caesar ..... Matthew 22:21
Call of God ..... Matthew 20:16
Called ones ..... Matthew 22:14
Capital and labor ..... Matthew 20:1–15
Capital punishment ..... Matthew 26:52
Care of God ..... Matthew 6:30, 33
Caution ..... Mark 4:24
Celibacy ..... Matthew 19;11,12
Character ..... John 1:47
Charity ..... Luke 12:33
Cheating ..... Mark 10:19
Chosen ..... Matthew 22:14
Church ..... Matthew 18:17
Circumcision ..... John 7:22, 23
Cleansing ..... John 15:3
Coin ..... Matthew 22:19–21
Coldness ..... Matthew 24:12
Communication ..... Luke 24:17
Compassion ..... Matthew 15:32
Luke 10:33
Compromise ..... Matthew 5:25,26

Conceit ..... Luke 18:10–12
Conduct, Christian ..... Matthew 5:16
Confessing Christ ..... Matthew 10:32, 33
Confession of sin ..... Luke 18:13, 14
Confidence ..... Mark 10:24
Conflict ..... Matthew 10:34–36
Conscience ..... John 8:7–9
Contention ..... Matthew 18:15–17
Contentment ..... John 6:43
Conversion ..... Matthew 13:15
Convict ..... John 16:8
Corruption, moral ..... Luke 11:39
Courage ..... Matthew 9:22
Covenant ..... Mark 14:24
Coveting ..... Mark 7:21, 22
Cross-bearing ..... Matthew 10:38
Crucifixion ..... Luke 9:22
Cup of water ..... Matthew 10:42

Dancing ..... Luke 15:25–27
Daniel ..... Matthew 24:15
Darkness ..... Luke 11:35
David ..... Matthew 12:3
Day ..... John 11:9
Deaf ..... Matthew 13:13–15
Death ..... Luke 9:22
John 8:51
Debts ..... Matthew 18:24
Deceivers ..... Matthew 24:4, 5
Decision ..... Matthew 6:24
Defilement ..... Matthew 15:11, 18, 19
Devil ..... Matthew 13:38,39
Diligence ..... John 9:4
Disbelief ..... John 5:38
Discernment ..... Matthew 16:2, 3
Discipleship ..... Luke 14:33
Disputes ..... Mark 9:33, 34

Distress ..... Luke 21:23, 25
Divorce ..... Matthew 5:31, 32
Doctrine ..... Mark 7:7
Doubt ..... Matthew 21:21
Drunkard ..... Luke 7:34
Drunkenness ..... Luke 21:34
Dullness ..... Matthew 13:13
Duty ..... Luke 17:10
Dwelling places ..... John 14:2, 3

Earth ..... Matthew 5:18
Earthquakes ..... Mark 13:8
Economy ..... Matthew 15:37
John 16:12
Elect ..... Matthew 24:24, 31
Election ..... Matthew 25:34
Elijah ..... Matthew 17:11, 12
Employer ..... Matthew 20:1–16
Encouragement ..... Matthew 9:2
Endowments ..... Matthew 25:14, 15
Endurance ..... Matthew 10:22
Luke 21:19
Enemies ..... Matthew 5:43, 44
Eternal life ..... Matthew 19:29
Eternal sin ..... Mark 3:29
Etiquette ..... Luke 10:8
Evil ..... Matthew 15:19
Exaltation ..... Matthew 23:12
Example ..... John 13:15
Excuses ..... Luke 14:18–20
Extravagance ..... Luke 15:11–14

Fainting ..... Mark 8:2, 3
Faith ..... Matthew 6; 25
Mark 11:22
Luke 7:50
Faithfulness ..... Matthew 25:21

Faithlessness ..... Matthew 25:24–30
False prophets ..... Matthew 24:11
False witness ..... Matthew 19:18
Farm ..... Matthew 22:2–6
Fasting ..... Matthew 6:16–18
Faultfinding ..... Matthew 7:3–5
Faults ..... Matthew 18:15
Fear of God ..... Matthew 10:28
Feast ..... Luke 14:8
Feet washing ..... John 13:12–15
Fellowship ..... Matthew 8:11
Flattery ..... Luke 6:26
Flesh ..... John 6:53
Flock ..... Matthew 26:31
Following Christ ..... Matthew 10:37, 38
Food ..... Matthew 6:11
Matthew 6:25
John 6:27
Fool ..... Matthew 5:22
Formalism ..... Matthew 23:23–28
Forsaking all ..... Luke 14:33
Foxes ..... Luke 9:58
Friends ..... Luke 11:5–8
Frugality ..... John 6:12
Fruitfulness ..... Matthew 13:23
Fruitlessness ..... Luke 13:6–9

Generosity ..... Matthew 25:34–40
Gentiles ..... Matthew 10:5–7
Gentleness ..... Matthew 5:5
Giving ..... Luke 6:38
Gladness ..... Luke 15:32
Glorifying God ..... Matthew 5:16
Gluttony ..... Luke 21:34
God ..... Matthew 19:17, 26
Godlessness ..... John 5:42,44
Golden Rule ..... Matthew 7:12

Gospel ..... Luke 4:18
Grace ..... 2 Corinthians 12:9
Greatness ..... Matthew 5:19
Grumble ..... John 6:43
Guidance ..... John 16:13

Hairs numbered ..... Matthew 10:30
Hand of God ..... John 10:27–29
Happiness ..... Matthew 5:12
John 13:16, 17
Harlots ..... Matthew 21:31
Harvest ..... Matthew 9:37, 38
Hatred ..... John 15:18, 19
Healing ..... Matthew 10:7, 8
Mark 2:17
Heart ..... Matthew 13:19
Heaven ..... Luke 16:17
John 3:13
Hell ..... Matthew 5:22
Matthew 10:28
Helpless ..... John 6:44
Hireling ..... John 10:11–13
Holy Spirit ..... John 14:26
Home ..... Mark 5:19
Honesty ..... Luke 8:15
Mark 10:19
Honor of men ..... Matthew 6:2
Honor of parents ..... Matthew 15:3–6
Hospitality ..... Luke 14:12–14
Humility ..... John 13:14
Hunger, spiritual ..... Luke 6:21
Matthew 5:6
Hypocrisy ..... Matthew 6:5
Luke 6:42

Ignorance ..... Matthew 22:29
Immortality..... Matthew 25:46
John 11:25, 26

Impartiality of God ..... Matthew 5:45
Inconsistency ..... Matthew 7:3–5
Luke 6:41, 42
Indecision ..... Luke 9:62
Indifference ..... Matthew 24:12
Industry ..... John 4:36
Infidelity ..... John 3:18
Influence..... Matthew 5:13
Ingratitude ..... Luke 17:17, 18
Innocence ..... Matthew 10:16
Insincerity ..... Luke 16:15
Inspiration ..... Luke 12:12
Instability ..... Matthew 7:26, 27
Instruction ..... John 6:45
Insufficiency ..... Mark 10:21
Integrity ..... Luke 16:10
Intercession ..... John 17:9
Investment ..... Matthew 6:19, 20

Jealousy ..... Luke 15:25–30
John the Baptist ..... Luke 7:24–28
Jonah ..... Matthew 12:39–41
Joy ..... Matthew 25:21
Luke 15:7, 10
Judge not ..... Matthew 7:1, 2
Judgment ..... Matthew 11:24
Judgment day ..... Matthew 25:31–46
Justice..... John 5:30
Justification, self ..... Luke 16:15

Killing ..... Matthew 5:21, 22
Kindness ..... Luke 10:30–35
Kingdom..... Luke 7:28
John 18:36
Kiss ..... Luke 7:45
Knowledge..... John 8:31, 32

Labor ..... Matthew 20:1–14
Laughter ..... Luke 6:21
Law ..... Luke 16:16
Lawsuit ..... Matthew 5:25, 40
Lawyers ..... Luke 11:46
Leaven ..... Matthew 16:16
Luke 13:20, 21
Lending ..... Luke 6:34, 35
Lepers ..... Matthew 10:7, 8
Levite ..... Luke 10:30–32
Liars ..... John 8:44, 45
Liberality ..... Luke 6:30–38
Liberty ..... Luke 4:18
Life ..... Matthew 6:25
John 5:40
Light ..... Luke 11:33
John 8:12
Living water ..... John 4:10
Log ..... Luke 6:41, 42
Loneliness ..... John 16:32
Lord's Supper ..... Matthew 26:26–29
Loss of soul ..... Matthew 16:25, 26
Lost opportunity ..... Matthew 25:7–12
Love ..... Matthew 22:37–40
Lukewarmness ..... Matthew 26:40, 41
Lunatic ..... Matthew 17:14, 15
Lust ..... Mark 4:18, 19

Magistrates ..... Luke 12:11, 58
Mammon ..... Matthew 6:24
Marriage ..... Matthew 19:4–6
Mark 12:25
Martyrdom ..... John 16:1–3
Mary's choice ..... Luke 10:41, 42
Memorial ..... Matthew 26:13
Mercy ..... Matthew 5:7
Luke 16:24

Minister ..... Luke 10:2
Miracles ..... Matthew 12:28
Money lender, creditor ..... Luke 7:41, 42
Moses ..... Matthew 19:8'
Moses' Law ..... John 7:19
Mother ..... Matthew 10:37
Mourn ..... Matthew 5:4
Murder ..... Matthew 15:19
Mysteries of Heaven ..... Matthew 13:11

Narrow way ..... Matthew 7:13, 14
Neglect ..... Luke 12:47
Neighbor ..... Matthew 19:19
Neutrality ..... Matthew 12:30
New birth ..... John 3:3, 5–8
Noah ..... Luke 17:26, 27

Oath ..... Matthew 5:33–37
Obedience ..... Matthew 12:50
Offering ..... Matthew 5:25
Offerings..... Luke 21:3, 4
Opportunity ..... Matthew 5:25

Parables ..... Mark 4:11, 12
Paradise ..... Luke 23:43
Pardoning ..... Luke 6:37
Parents ..... Matthew 10:21
Patriotism ..... Matthew 22:21
Peace ..... Mark 9:50
Peacemakers ..... Matthew 5:9
Penitence ..... Luke 18:13
Perception ..... John 8:43
Perfection ..... Matthew 5:48
Persecution..... Matt 24:9
Perseverance ..... Matthew 10:22
Pharisaism ..... Matthew 23:2–33
Pharisee and tax collector..... Luke 18:10–14

Pharisees ..... Matthew 5:20
Philanthropy ..... Luke 11:41
Physician ..... Matthew 9:12
Piety ..... John 1:47
Pleasing God ..... John 8:29
Pleasures ..... Luke 8:14
Poison ..... Mark 16:17, 18
Poll tax ..... Matthew 22:19–21
Polygamy ..... Matthew 19:8, 9
Poor ..... Mark 14:7
Power ..... Matthew 6:13
Prayer ..... Matthew 7:7–11
Matthew 6:9–13
Preaching ..... Mark 16:15, 16
Procrastination ..... Matthew 25:3
Profit and loss ..... Matthew 16:26
Prophets ..... Matthew 10:41
Proselyte ..... Luke 23:15
Protection ..... Luke 18:3
Providence ..... Matthew 6:25–30
Prudence ..... Matthew 10:16–20
Punishment ..... Matthew 21:41
Purity ..... Matthew 5:8

Ransom ..... Matthew 20:28
Reaping ..... John 4:35–38
Receiving Christ ..... Mark 9:37
Reconciliation ..... Matthew 5:23, 24
Regeneration ..... Matthew 19:28
Rejecting Christ ..... John 3:18
Rejoicing ..... Luke 10:20
Release ..... Luke 4:18
Religion ..... Mark 7:6–8
Matthew 25:34–36
Repentance ..... Matthew 11:21
Luke 13:28
Reproof ..... Matthew 11:21–23

Resignation ..... Matthew 26:39
Responsibility ..... Luke 12:47, 48
Rest ..... Matthew 26:45
Matthew 11:28–30
Resurrection ..... John 6:40
Retaliation ..... Mat. 5:39–44
Retribution ..... Matthew 23:34, 35
Reward ..... Matthew 10:42
Riches ..... Mark 4:19
Righteousness ..... Matthew 5:6, 20
Robbers ..... Luke 10:30
John 10:1
Robbery ..... Matthew 23:25

Sabbath ..... Matthew 12:5–8
Sackcloth ..... Matthew 11:21
Sacrifice ..... Matthew 12:7
Sacrilege ..... Mat. 12:7
Sadducees ..... Matthew 16:6
Salt ..... Matthew 5:13
Mark 9:50
Salvation ..... Luke 19:19
John 4:22
Samaritan ..... Luke 10:30–35
Sanctification ..... John 17:17
Satan ..... Matthew 4:10
Mark 4:15
Scripture ..... Matthew 21:42
Luke 4:21
Secrecy ..... Luke 12:2, 3
Security ..... Luke 6:47, 48
Seduction ..... Mark 13:22
Seeking the kingdom ..... Matthew 6:19, 20
Self-condemnation ..... Matthew 23:29–32
Luke 12:20–24
Self-control ..... Matthew 5:21
Self-deception ..... Luke 12:16–21

Self-denial ..... Matthew 16:24–26
Self-exaltation ..... Matthew 23:12
Self-examination ..... Matthew 7:3–5
Selfishness ..... Luke 6; 32–35
Self-righteousness ..... Matthew 23:23–27
Self-sacrifice ..... Matthew 16:25
Serpents ..... Matthew 23:33
John 3:14
Service ..... Luke 22:27
Sheep ..... Luke 15:4–7
Shepherd ..... John 10:1–18
Sickness ..... Matthew 10:8
Signs ..... John 4:48
Luke 11:16
Silence ..... Matthew 17:9
Sin ..... John 8:34
Matthew 26:28
Sincerity ..... Matthew 5:13–16
Skepticism ..... John 20:27, 29
Slaves ..... Matthew 18:23
John 15:15
Sleep ..... Mark 4:26, 27
Mark 13:35, 36
Slothfulness ..... Matthew 25:26–30
Son of Man ..... Luke 9:22
Sorrow ..... Matthew 19:22
John 16:6
Soul ..... Matthew 10:28
Luke 12:19, 20
Soul winners ..... Matthew 4:19
Sowing ..... Mark 4:14
Speech ..... John 8:43
Spirit ..... Matthew 26:41
Mark 5:8
Statement ..... Matthew 5:37
Steadfastness ..... Matthew 10:22
Stealing ..... Matthew 19:18

Steward ..... Luke 12:42, 43
Luke 16:1–8
Stewardship ..... Luke 19:13–27
Stomach ..... Matthew 15:17
Strife ..... Luke 22:24
Stubbornness ..... John 5:40
Stumbling block ..... Matthew 23:13
Submission ..... Matthew 26:39, 42
Suffering ..... Matthew 26:38
Supper, The Lord's ..... Luke 22:14–20
Swearing ..... Matthew 23:16–22

Talents ..... Matthew 18:24
Taxes ..... Matthew 22:19–21
Tax collectors ..... Matthew 5:46, 47
Teaching ..... Matthew 28:19, 20
John 13:13–15
Temperance ..... Luke 21:34
Temptations ..... Matthew 4:1–11
Luke 8:13
Thieves ..... Matthew 6:19
John 10:1, 8
Timidness ..... Mark 4:40
Tithes ..... Luke 18:11, 12
Traditions ..... Mark 7:9, 13
Transgressions ..... Matthew 15:2
Treasures ..... Matthew 6:19–21
Tribulation ..... Matthew 24:9
John 16:33
Truth ..... John 14:6

Unbelievers ..... Luke 12:46
Uncharitableness ..... John 7:24
Unchastity ..... Matthew 5:31, 32
Uncleanness ..... Matthew 23:27
Unity ..... John 17:20, 21
Unpardonable sin ..... Matthew 12:31, 32

Vengeance ..... Matthew 5:39, 40
Vine ..... John 15:1, 4, 5
Visions ..... Matthew 17:9

Walks of life ..... John 12:35
War ..... Matthew 24:26
Watchfulness ..... Matthew 24:42, 44
Luke 12:37–40
Wedding ..... Luke 14:8–10
Widow ..... Mark 12:43, 44
Wine ..... Luke 5:37–39
Wisdom ..... Luke 21:15
Witness ..... John 8:14
Witness, false ..... Matthew 19:18
Witnessing ..... Acts 1:8
Wives ..... Luke 14:20, 26
Worker ..... Matthew 10:10
Worldliness ..... Luke 21:34
Worm ..... Mark 9:43–48
Worries of the world ..... Matthew 13:22
Worship Matthew4:10

Yoke ..... Matthew 11:28, 29

Zacchaeus ..... Luke 19:5
Zeal ..... John 2:17

What Just Happened?

MULTIPLE CHOICE

1. **Which of the following occurred as a result of Adam and Eve's sin?**
   - **A.** They experienced knowledge of evil.
   - **B.** They experienced shame and guilt.
   - **C.** They feared God's presence.
   - **D.** all of the above
   - **E.** The shekel market fell 200 points.

ANSWERS p. 243

2. **What happened immediately after Adam and Eve made clothes for themselves?**
   - **A.** They went out of the garden.
   - **B.** They heard God walking in the garden.
   - **C.** They went out of style.
   - **D.** They hid in the trees.

3. **God sent The Flood to cover the earth because:**
   - **A.** The wickedness of man was great in the earth, and all his thoughts were evil.
   - **B.** The people of Ur hated God.
   - **C.** The people of the earth laughed in the face of his warnings.
   - **D.** Simon said to.

4. **How long did The Flood cover the earth?**
   - **A.** 2 years
   - **B.** too long
   - **C.** 5 months
   - **D.** 40 days

SHORT ANSWER

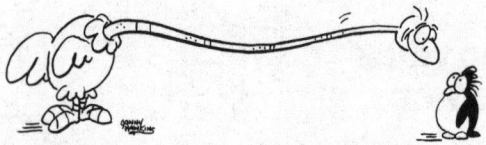

1. The tower of Babel was built to do what?

_____

2. How did God punish the men who built the tower? _____

3. What event sparked God's destruction of Sodom?

_____

_____

4. Who pulled Lot out of the city of Sodom?

_____

_____

MATCHING

1. Abraham
2. Samson
3. Ruth
4. David
5. Lot
6. Nehemiah
7. Bill and Ted
8. Hosea
9. Rahab
10. Esther

a. escaped burning city with wife and daughters
b. hid spies in her home
c. rebuilt a city wall
d. was asked to sacrifice his son
e. had an excellent adventure
f. won a beauty pagent
g. destroyed a house full of Philistines
h. married a prostitute
i. murdered a soldier
j. met her husband while working in the fields

FILL IN THE BLANKS

1. Rahab lived in _____.
2. Ehud killed this king: _____.
3. _____ had Uriah killed.
4. This city was raided by Israel: _____.
5. Ruth's first mother-in-law was _____.

ANSWERS p. 244

6. The Philistines stole this important item from the Israelites: _____.

7. This man ran from God to Tarshish: _____.

8. Lot's wife turned into _____.

WORD BANK

Naomi	Ark	Sand	Eglon
Jonah	Bezek	Salt	Salt
Jericho	David	Danny	Rahab

PUT THE FOLLOWING IN ORDER

Plagues

1. Flies
2. Livestock died
3. Darkness over the land
4. Water turned to blood
5. Hail storm
6. Frogs
7. Locusts

8. Boils
9. Death of the first born
10. Lice

Ten Commandments

1. Remember the Sabbath Day and keep it holy
2. Do not commit adultery
3. Have no other gods before Me
4. Do not covet
5. Honor your father and mother
6. Have no graven images
7. Do not murder
8. Do not lie
9. Do not take God's name in vain
10. Do not steal

ANSWERS p. 245

HOW ABOUT THAT!

A man claimed he saw Noah's ark on Mt. Ararat in 1908, and today a picture of it exists.

TRUE OR FALSE

1. Passover commemorates Israel's deliverance from Egypt and is a reminder that Christ spared the first born.

2. The Feast of Unleavened Bread is symbolized by communion in modern days.

3. The Day of Firstfruits dedicated the firstfruits of the wheat harvest.

4. The Feast of Pentecost, Harvest, and Weeks is symbolized by the outpouring of the Holy Spirit.

5. The Day of Trumpets commemorates Israel's defeat of Jericho.

6. The Day of Atonement is fulfilled in Christ's crucifixion.

7. The Feast of Tabernacles commemorates God's deliverance.

8. The Feast of Purim was held to recognize the goodness God bestowed on his people because of their sacrifices.

FILL IN THE BLANKS

1. Because Sarai lived in Pharaoh's house claiming to be Abram's sister, God sent _____ on Pharaoh's house.

2. What did Joseph's brothers find in their sacks of grain? _____

3. The people of Israel plundered the Egyptians by having every woman ask her neighbor for articles of _____ and _____ and _____.

4. Pharaoh's magicians could imitate _____ of Moses' miracles.

5. Why did the Israelites call the food sent to them in the desert manna? _____

6. Moses burned the golden calf, ground it into powder, poured it on the water and made the Israelites _____ _____.

ANSWERS p. 246

WORD BANK

Because it means "what is it?"

locusts two drink it

none copper his own money

silver gold worms clothing

Because it was white plagues

MULTIPLE CHOICE

1. **Moses did what to part the Red Sea?**
   - **A.** commanded the waters to part
   - **B.** hit it with a rod
   - **C.** sang "Pharaoh, Pharaoh, whoa, oh, Let my people go!"
   - **D.** lifted up rod and stretched out hand

Top Ten Feasts the Israelites Didn't Celebrate

10. Feast of Juicyfruits
9. Combover
8. Feast of Tubas
7. Feast of Harems
6. Feast of Winnebagos
5. Feast of day-old doughnuts
4. Feast of Garlic Bread
3. Day of Ham
2. Day of Organ Donors
1. Wash A Sauna

2. **How many people exited Egypt with Moses?**
   A. six hundred men with their families
   B. six thousand men with their families
   C. six hundred thousand men with their families
   D. none

3. **Where was the Promised Land?**
   A. the mountains of the Amorites all the way to the land of the Canaanites and Lebanon as far as the river Euphrates
   B. the mountains of the Amorites all the way to the land of the Canaanites but not beyond, for that is the land of the pagan peoples
   C. the great Smokey Mountains, all the way to the Adirondacks of New England
   D. all the land of the Canaanites, and no more

4. **What flowed in the Promised Land?**
   A. milk
   B. honey
   C. hair
   D. manna

5. **Which of the spies who entered Canaan thought the Israelites should enter?**
   A. Moses and Aaron
   B. Joshua and Caleb
   C. Rocky and Bullwinkle
   D. Reuben and Igal

6. **Why did the Israelites go to war with the Benjaminites?**

A. They kept raising the price of oil
B. They pillaged the Israelite's land
C. A Levite's concubine was raped
D. They stole the ark of the covenant

7. **What was Samson's riddle about?**
   A. a lion
   B. a bear
   C. I don't know, but it brought the house down.
   D. a Philistine

8. **Which of the following were Delilah's attempts to weaken Samson?**
   A. bound him with fresh bowstrings
   B. tied him with weathered ropes
   C. wove five locks of his hair
   D. took away his Nautilus system

ANSWERS p. 247

TRUE OR FALSE

1. David put only one stone in his bag when he prepared to fight Goliath.

2. Saul gave his daughter Michal to another man while she was still married to David.

3. A medium brought Samuel back from the dead to speak to Saul.

4. David built a temple.

5. Assyria captured the northern kingdom of Israel.

6. Both Elijah and Elisha raised boys from the dead.

7. The first thing the Israelites built when returning from captivity in Babylon was a new temple.

8. Israel wanted a king so that they could be like other nations and fight.

9. Solomon had a hard time getting dates.

10. Jonah stayed in the fish for forty days and nights.

MULTIPLE CHOICE

1. **The wise men saw the star how many times?**
   - **A.** one
   - **B.** two
   - **C.** infinity
   - **D.** four

2. **How did Joseph know that God did not want him to take Jesus back to Judea when the family returned from Egypt?**
   - **A.** dream
   - **B.** Mary knew
   - **C.** when he tried to go, his feet caught on fire
   - **D.** finger writing on the wall

3. **Who saw the Holy Spirit descend on Jesus like a dove?**
   - **A.** Jesus
   - **B.** all who had eyes to see

C. Jesus and John the Baptist
D. members of the local birdwatchers society

4. The centurion said to Jesus:
A. "Only speak a word, and my servant will be healed."
B. "Please, come and heal my servant."
C. "You complete me."
D. "Your will be done."

5. What name completes this prophecy: "Out of _____ I called my Son."
A. Mary
B. Bethlehem
C. Africa
D. Egypt

ANSWERS p. 248

6. What was Jesus doing when the tempest arose around the boat?
A. preaching
B. eating
C. sleeping
D. knitting

7. What interrupted Jesus on his way to heal Jairus's daughter?

Q. What was the first thing Adam and Eve did when they were kicked out of the Garden of Eden?

A. Raised Cain!

A. a hemorrhaging woman
B. a demon-possessed man
C. a breaking news report
D. a centurion

8. **Whose Son did the two blind men who were following Jesus say that He was?**
   A. God's
   B. David's
   C. Joseph's
   D. Daniel-son

UNSCRAMBLE

1. Gansirfatruniot
2. Recrusretnoi
3. Lumacteima Peretonic
4. Ficurxnioci
5. Salt Puresp
6. Tesoctnep
7. Siarminoys Njoruyes
8. Lapu febreo het Hendrsani
9. Toscdowok
10. Dingdwe Puesrp fo het Ambl

ANSWERS p. 249

Q. Who was the best high-jumper in the Bible?
A. Jesus, He cleared the temple.

ANSWERS TO: WHAT JUST HAPPENED?

MULTIPLE CHOICE

#	ANSWER	REFERENCE
1.	d	Genesis 3:7–8
2.	b	Genesis 3:8
3.	a	Genesis 6:5
4.	c	Genesis 7:11–8:4

SHORT ANSWER

#	ANSWER	REFERENCE
1.	to make a name for themselves	Genesis 11:4
2.	confused their language	Genesis 11:8
3.	the men of the city desired to rape the angels staying in Lot's home	Genesis 19:1–11
4.	the angels pulled Lot, his wife and two daughters out	Genesis 19:16

MATCHING

#	ANSWER	REFERENCE
1.	d	Genesis 22
2.	g	Judges 16
3.	j	Ruth 2
4.	i	2 Samuel 11
5.	a	Genesis 19
6.	c	Nehemiah 3
7.	e	(movie)
8.	h	Hosea 1
9.	b	Joshua 2
10.	f	Esther 2

FILL IN THE BLANKS

#	ANSWER	REFERENCE
1.	Jericho	Joshua 2
2.	Eglon	Judges 3
3.	David	2 Samuel 11
4.	Bezek	Judges 1
5.	Naomi	Ruth 1
6.	Ark	1 Samuel 5

#	ANSWER	REFERENCE
7.	Jonah	Jonah 1
8.	Salt	Genesis 19:26

PUT THE FOLLOWING IN ORDER

#	ANSWER	REFERENCE
1.	Plagues: 4, 6, 10, 1, 2, 8, 5, 7, 3, 9	Exodus 7–12
2.	10 Commandments: 3, 6, 9, 1, 5, 7, 2, 10, 8, 4	Exodus 20

TRUE OR FALSE

#	ANSWER	REFERENCE
1.	True	Exodus 12:27
2.	False; True Church	John 6, 1 Cor. 5
3.	False; Barley	Leviticus 23
4.	True	Exodus 23, Lev. 23, Num. 28, Deut. 16, Acts 2

TRUE OR FALSE—cont'd

#	ANSWER	REFERENCE
5.	False; Consecrates	Leviticus 23, Num. 10; Sabbatical Month
6.	True	Hebrews 9
7.	True	Leviticus 23
8.	False	Deliverence from genocide during Esther's time—Esther 9

FILL IN THE BLANKS

#	ANSWER	REFERENCE
1.	plagues	Genesis 12:7
2.	his own money	Genesis 42:35
3.	silver, gold, and clothing	Exodus 3:22
4.	two	Exodus 7–8
5.	what is it?	Exodus 16:15
6.	drink it	Exodus 32:20

MULTIPLE CHOICE

#	ANSWER	REFERENCE
1.	d	Exodus 14:16
2.	c	Exodus 12:37
3.	a	Deuteronomy 1:5–8
4.	a,b	Exodus 3:8
5.	b	Numbers 14
6.	c	Judges 20
7.	a	Judges 14
8.	a	Judges 16

TRUE OR FALSE

#	ANSWER	REFERENCE
1.	False; five	1 Samuel 17:40
2.	True	1 Samuel 25:44
3.	True	1 Samuel 28:11–19
4.	False	2 Samuel 7:1–7
5.	True	2 Kings 17:5–6
6.	True	2 Kings 4, 1 Kings 17

TRUE OR FALSE—cont'd

#	ANSWER	REFERENCE
7.	False; altar	Ezra 3:2
8.	True	1 Samuel 8:20
9.	False	
10.	False; three days and nights	Jonah 1:17

MULTIPLE CHOICE

#	ANSWER	REFERENCE
1.	b	Matthew 2:2,9
2.	a	Matthew 2:2
3.	c	Matthew 3:16, John 1:32
4.	a	Matthew 8:8
5.	d	Matthew 2:15
6.	c	Matthew 8:24
7.	a	Matthew 9:20
8.	b	Matthew 9:27

UNSCRAMBLE

#	ANSWER
1.	Transfiguration
2.	Resurrection
3.	Immaculate Reception
4.	Crucifixion
5.	Last Supper
6.	Pentecost
7.	Missionary Journeys
8.	Paul before the Sanhedrin
9.	Woodstock
10.	Wedding Supper of the Lamb

PROPHECIES OF THE MESSIAH FULFILLED IN JESUS CHRIST

Presented Here in Their Order of Fulfillment

SEED OF A WOMAN

Prophecy Genesis 3:15
"And I will put enmity between you and the woman, and between your seed and her Seed; He shall bruise your head, and you shall bruise His heel."

Fulfilled Galatians 4:4
But when the fullness of the time had come, God sent forth His Son, born of a woman, born under the law.

SEED OF ABRAHAM

Prophecy Genesis 12:3
"I will bless those who bless you, and I will curse him who curses you; and in you all the families of the earth shall be blessed."

Fulfilled Matthew 1:1
The book of the genealogy of Jesus Christ, the Son of David, the Son of Abraham.

SEED OF ISAAC

Prophecy Genesis 17:19
Then God said: "No, Sarah your wife shall bear you a son, and you shall call his name Isaac; I will establish My covenant with him for an everlasting covenant, *and* with his descendants after him."

Fulfilled Luke 3:34
The son of Jacob, *the son* of Isaac, *the son* of Abraham, *the son* of Terah, *the son* of Nahor.

SEED OF JACOB

Prophecy Numbers 24:17
"I see Him, but not now; I behold Him, but not near; a Star shall come out of Jacob; a Scepter shall rise out of Israel, and batter the brow of Moab, and destroy all the sons of tumult."

Fulfilled Matthew 1:2
Abraham begot Isaac, Isaac begot Jacob, and Jacob begot Judah and his brothers.

FROM THE TRIBE OF JUDAH

Prophecy Genesis 49:10
"The scepter shall not depart from Judah, nor a lawgiver from between his feet, until Shiloh comes; and to Him *shall be* the obedience of the people."

Fulfilled Luke 3:33
The son of Amminadab, *the son* of Ram, *the son* of Hezron, *the son* of Perez, *the son* of Judah.

HEIR TO THE THRONE OF DAVID

Prophecy Isaiah 9:7
Of the increase of *His* government and peace *there will be* no end, upon the throne of David and over His kingdom, to order it and establish it with judgment and justice from that time forward, even forever. The zeal of the LORD of hosts will perform this.

Fulfilled Luke 1:32, 33
"He will be great, and will be called the Son of the Highest; and the Lord God will give Him the throne of His father David.

"And He will reign over the house of Jacob forever, and of His kingdom there will be no end."

BORN IN BETHLEHEM

Prophecy Micah 5:2
"But you, Bethlehem Ephrathah, *though* you are little among the thousands of Judah, *yet* out of you shall come forth to Me the One to be ruler in Israel, whose goings forth *have been* from of old, from everlasting."

Fulfilled Luke 2:4, 5, 7
And Joseph also went up from Galilee, out of the city of Nazareth, into Judea, to the city of David, which is called Bethlehem, because he was of the house and lineage of David, to be registered with Mary, his betrothed wife, who was with child.

And she brought forth her firstborn Son, and wrapped Him in swaddling cloths, and laid Him in a manger, because there was no room for them in the inn.

TIME FOR HIS BAPTISM

Prophecy Daniel 9:25
"Know therefore and understand, *that* from the going forth of the command to restore and build Jerusalem until Messiah the Prince, *there shall be* seven weeks and sixty-two weeks; the street shall be built again, and the wall, even in troublesome times."

Fulfilled Luke 3:21, 22
Now when all the people were baptized, it came to pass that Jesus also was baptized; and while He prayed, the heaven was opened.

And the Holy Spirit descended in bodily form like a dove

upon Him, and a voice came from heaven which said, "You are My beloved Son; in You I am well pleased."

TO BE BORN OF A VIRGIN

Prophecy Isaiah 7:14
"Therefore the Lord Himself will give you a sign: Behold, the virgin shall conceive and bear a Son, and shall call His name Immanuel."

Fulfilled Luke 1:26, 27, 30, 31
Now in the sixth month the angel Gabriel was sent by God to a city of Galilee named Nazareth, to a virgin betrothed to a man whose name was Joseph, of the house of David. The virgin's name *was* Mary.

Then the angel said to her, "Do not be afraid, Mary, for you have found favor with God.

"And behold, you will conceive in your womb and bring forth a Son, and shall call His name JESUS."

SLAUGHTER OF THE INNOCENTS

Prophecy Jeremiah 31:15
Thus says the LORD: "A voice was heard in Ramah, lamentation *and* bitter weeping, Rachel weeping for her children, refusing to be comforted for her children, because they *are* no more."

Fulfilled Matthew 2:16–18
Then Herod, when he saw that he was deceived by the wise men, was exceedingly angry; and he sent forth and put to death all the male children who were in Bethlehem and in all its districts, from two years old and under, according to the time which he had determined from the wise men.

Then was fulfilled what was spoken by Jeremiah the prophet, saying:

"A voice was heard in Ramah, lamentation, weeping, and

great mourning, Rachel weeping for her children, refusing to be comforted, because they were no more."

FLIGHT TO EGYPT

Prophecy Hosea 11:1
"When Israel *was* a child, I loved him, and out of Egypt I called My son."

Fulfilled Matthew 2:14, 15
When he arose, he took the young Child and His mother by night and departed for Egypt, and was there until the death of Herod, that it might be fulfilled which was spoken by the Lord through the prophet, saying, *"Out of Egypt I called My Son."*

PRECEDED BY A FORERUNNER

Prophecy Malachi 3:1
"Behold, I send My messenger, and he will prepare the way before Me. And the Lord, whom you seek, will suddenly come to His temple, even the Messenger of the covenant, in whom you delight. Behold, He is coming," says the LORD of hosts.

Fulfilled Luke 7:24, 27
When the messengers of John had departed, He began to speak to the multitudes concerning John: "What did you go out into the wilderness to see? A reed shaken by the wind?

"This is *he* of whom it is written: *'Behold, I send My messenger before Your face, who will prepare Your way before You.'*

DECLARED THE SON OF GOD

Prophecy Psalm 2:7
"I will declare the decree: the LORD has said to Me, 'You *are* My Son, today I have begotten You.'"

Fulfilled Matthew 3:17
And suddenly a voice *came* from heaven, saying, "This is My beloved Son, in whom I am well pleased."

GALILEAN MINISTRY

Prophecy Isaiah 9:1, 2
Nevertheless the gloom *will* not *be* upon her who *is* distressed, as when at first He lightly esteemed the land of Zebulun and the land of Naphtali, and afterward more heavily oppressed *her, by* the way of the sea, beyond the Jordan, in Galilee of the Gentiles.

The people who walked in darkness have seen a great light; those who dwelt in the land of the shadow of death, upon them a light has shined.

Fulfilled Matthew 4:13–16
And leaving Nazareth, He came and dwelt in Capernaum, which is by the sea, in the regions of Zebulun and Naphtali, that it might be fulfilled which was spoken by Isaiah the prophet, saying:

"The land of Zebulun and the land of Naphtali, the way of the sea, beyond the Jordan, Galilee of the Gentiles: the people who sat in darkness saw a great light, And upon those who sat in the region and shadow of death light has dawned."

A PROPHET

Prophecy Deuteronomy 18:15
"The LORD your God will raise up for you a Prophet like me from your midst, from your brethren. Him you shall hear."

Fulfilled Acts 3:20, 22
"And that He may send Jesus Christ, who was preached to you before.

"For Moses truly said to the fathers, '*The LORD your God*

will raise up for you a Prophet like me from your brethren. Him you shall hear in all things, whatever He says to you."'

TO HEAL THE BROKENHEARTED

Prophecy Isaiah 61:1, 2
"The Spirit of the Lord GOD *is* upon Me, because the LORD has anointed Me to preach good tidings to the poor; He has sent Me to heal the brokenhearted, to proclaim liberty to the captives, and the opening of the prison to *those who are* bound; to proclaim the acceptable year of the LORD, and the day of vengeance of our God; to comfort all who mourn."

Fulfilled Luke 4:18, 19
"The Spirit of the LORD is upon Me, because He has anointed Me to preach the gospel to the poor. He has sent Me to heal the brokenhearted, to preach deliverance to the captives and recovery of sight to the blind, to set at liberty those who are oppressed, to preach the acceptable year of the LORD."

REJECTED BY HIS OWN PEOPLE, THE JEWS

Prophecy Isaiah 53:3
He is despised and rejected by men, a man of sorrows and acquainted with grief. And we hid, as it were, *our* faces from Him; He was despised, and we did not esteem Him.

Fulfilled John 1:11
He came to His own, and His own did not receive Him.

Luke 23:18
And they all cried out at once, saying, "Away with this *Man,* and release to us Barabbas."

PRIEST AFTER ORDER OF MELCHIZEDEK

Prophecy Psalm 110:4
The LORD has sworn and will not relent, "You *are* a priest forever according to the order of Melchizedek."

Fulfilled Hebrews 5:5, 6
So also Christ did not glorify Himself to become High Priest, *but it* was He who said to Him: *"You are My Son, today I have begotten You."*

As *He* also *says* in another *place: "You are a priest forever according to the order of Melchizedek."*

TRIUMPHAL ENTRY

Prophecy Zechariah 9:9
"Rejoice greatly, O daughter of Zion! Shout, O daughter of Jerusalem! Behold, your King is coming to you; He *is* just and having salvation, lowly and riding on a donkey, a colt, the foal of a donkey."

Fulfilled Mark 11:7, 9, 11
Then they brought the colt to Jesus and threw their garments on it, and He sat on it.

Then those who went before and those who followed cried out, saying: "Hosanna! *'Blessed is He who comes in the name of the LORD!'"*

And Jesus went into Jerusalem and into the temple. So when He had looked around at all things, as the hour was already late, He went out to Bethany with the twelve.

BETRAYED BY A FRIEND

Prophecy Psalm 41:9
Even my own familiar friend in whom I trusted, who ate my bread, has lifted up *his* heel against me.

Fulfilled Luke 22:47, 48
And while He was still speaking, behold, a multitude; and he who was called Judas, one of the twelve, went before them and drew near to Jesus to kiss Him.

But Jesus said to him, "Judas, are you betraying the Son of Man with a kiss?"

SOLD FOR THIRTY PIECES OF SILVER

Prophecy Zechariah 11:12
Then I said to them, "If it is agreeable to you, give *me* my wages; and if not, refrain." So they weighed out for my wages thirty *pieces* of silver.

Fulfilled Matthew 26:15
And said, "What are you willing to give me if I deliver Him to you?" And they counted out to him thirty pieces of silver.

ACCUSED BY FALSE WITNESSES

Prophecy Psalm 35:11
Fierce witnesses rise up; they ask me *things* that I do not know.

Fulfilled Mark 14:57, 58
And some rose up and bore false witness against Him, saying, "We heard Him say, 'I will destroy this temple that *is* made with hands, and within three days I will build another made without hands.'"

SILENT TO ACCUSATIONS

Prophecy Isaiah 53:7
He was oppressed and He was afflicted, yet He opened not His mouth; He was led as a lamb to the slaughter, and as a sheep before its shearers is silent, so He opened not His mouth.

Fulfilled Mark 15:4, 5
Then Pilate asked Him again, saying, "Do You answer nothing? See how many things they testify against You!"
But Jesus still answered nothing, so that Pilate marveled.

SPAT UPON AND SMITTEN

Prophecy Isaiah 50:6
I gave My back to those who struck *Me*, and My cheeks to those who plucked out the beard; I did not hide My face from shame and spitting.

Fulfilled Matthew 26:67
Then they spat in His face and beat Him; and others struck *Him* with the palms of their hands.

HATED WITHOUT REASON

Prophecy Psalm 35:19
Let them not rejoice over me who are wrongfully my enemies; Nor let them wink with the eye who hate me without a cause.

Fulfilled John 15:24, 25
"If I had not done among them the works which no one else did, they would have no sin; but now they have seen and also hated both Me and My Father.

"But *this happened* that the word might be fulfilled which is written in their law, *'They hated Me without a cause.'*"

VICARIOUS SACRIFICE

Prophecy Isaiah 53:5
But He *was* wounded for our transgressions, *He was* bruised for our iniquities; the chastisement for our peace *was* upon Him, and by His stripes we are healed.

Fulfilled Romans 5:6, 8
For when we were still without strength, in due time Christ died for the ungodly.

But God demonstrates His own love toward us, in that while we were still sinners, Christ died for us.

CRUCIFIED WITH MALEFACTORS

Prophecy Isaiah 53:12
Therefore I will divide Him a portion with the great, and He shall divide the spoil with the strong, because He poured out His soul unto death, and He was numbered with the transgressors, and He bore the sin of many, And made intercession for the transgressors.

Fulfilled Mark 15:27, 28
With Him they also crucified two robbers, one on His right and the other on His left.

So the Scripture was fulfilled which says, *"And He was numbered with the transgressors."*

PIERCED THROUGH HANDS AND FEET

Prophecy Zechariah 12:10
"And I will pour on the house of David and on the inhabitants of Jerusalem the Spirit of grace and supplication; then they will look on Me whom they have pierced; they will mourn for Him as one mourns for *his* only *son,* and grieve for Him as one grieves for a firstborn."

Fulfilled John 20:27
Then He said to Thomas, "Reach your finger here, and look at My hands; and reach your hand *here,* and put *it* into My side. Do not be unbelieving, but believing."

SCORNED AND MOCKED

Prophecy Psalm 22:7, 8
All those who see Me laugh Me to scorn; they shoot out the lip, they shake the head, *saying,* "He trusted in the LORD, let Him rescue Him; let Him deliver Him, since He delights in Him!"

Fulfilled Luke 23:35
And the people stood looking on. But even the rulers with them sneered, saying, "He saved others; let Him save Himself if He is the Christ, the chosen of God."

GIVEN VINEGAR AND GALL

Prophecy Psalm 69:21
They also gave me gall for my food, and for my thirst they gave me vinegar to drink.

Fulfilled Matthew 27:34
They gave Him sour wine mingled with gall to drink. But when He had tasted *it,* He would not drink.

PRAYER FOR HIS ENEMIES

Prophecy Psalm 109:4
In return for my love they are my accusers, but I *give myself to* prayer.

Fulfilled Luke 23:34
Then Jesus said, "Father, forgive them, for they do not know what they do." And they divided His garments and cast lots.

SOLDIERS GAMBLED FOR HIS COAT

Prophecy Psalm 22:17, 18
I can count all My bones. They look *and* stare at Me.
They divide My garments among them, and for My clothing they cast lots.

Fulfilled Matthew 27:35, 36
Then they crucified Him, and divided His garments, casting lots, that it might be fulfilled which was spoken by the

prophet: *"They divided My garments among them, and for My clothing they cast lots."*

Sitting down, they kept watch over Him there.

NO BONES BROKEN

Prophecy Psalm 34:20

He guards all his bones; not one of them is broken

Fulfilled John 19:32, 33, 36

Then the soldiers came and broke the legs of the first and of the other who was crucified with Him.

But when they came to Jesus and saw that He was already dead, they did not break His legs.

For these things were done that the Scripture should be fulfilled, *"Not one of His bones shall be broken."*

HIS SIDE PIERCED

Prophecy Zechariah 12:10

"And I will pour on the house of David and on the inhabitants of Jerusalem the Spirit of grace and supplication; then they will look on Me whom they have pierced; they will mourn for Him as one mourns for *his* only *son,* and grieve for Him as one grieves for a firstborn."

Fulfilled John 19:34

But one of the soldiers pierced His side with a spear, and immediately blood and water came out.

BURIED WITH THE RICH

Prophecy Isaiah 53:9

And they made His grave with the wicked—but with the rich at His death, because He had done no violence, nor *was any* deceit in His mouth.

Fulfilled Matthew 27:57–60
Now when evening had come, there came a rich man from Arimathea, named Joseph, who himself had also become a disciple of Jesus.

This man went to Pilate and asked for the body of Jesus. Then Pilate commanded the body to be given to him.

And when Joseph had taken the body, he wrapped it in a clean linen cloth, and laid it in his new tomb which he had hewn out of the rock; and he rolled a large stone against the door of the tomb, and departed.

TO BE RESURRECTED

Prophecy Psalm 16:10
For You will not leave my soul in Sheol, nor will You allow Your Holy One to see corruption.

Psalm 49:15
But God will redeem my soul from the power of the grave, for He shall receive me. Selah

Fulfilled Mark 16:6, 7
But he said to them, "Do not be alarmed. You seek Jesus of Nazareth, who was crucified. He is risen! He is not here. See the place where they laid Him.

"But go *and* tell His disciples—and Peter—that He is going before you into Galilee; there you will see Him, as He said to you."

HIS ASCENSION TO GOD'S RIGHT HAND

Prophecy Psalm 68:18
You have ascended on high, You have led captivity captive; You have received gifts among men, even *among* the rebellious, that the LORD God might dwell *there.*

Fulfilled Mark 16:19

So then, after the Lord had spoken to them, He was received up into heaven, and sat down at the right hand of God.

1 Corinthians 15:4

And that He was buried, and that He rose again the third day according to the Scriptures.

Ephesians 4:8

Therefore He says: *"When He ascended on high, He led captivity captive, and gave gifts to men."*

When?

MULTIPLE CHOICE

1. **Which Sumerian city, ruled by King Meskalamdug and Queen Shub-ad, first emerged around 2700 B.C.?**
   A. Chaldee
   B. Shub-ad-dug-ad-doo!
   C. Ur
   D. Damascus

ANSWERS p. 284

2. **The first true pyramid was built in:**
   A. 2613 B.C.
   B. 1613 B.C.
   C. 613 B.C.
   D. LegoLand

3. **The Flood probably occurred around this date, putting it before the domestication of the horse, but after the domestication of the camel:**
   A. 3900 B.C.
   B. 2900 B.C.
   C. Prom 2000
   D. 1900 B.C.

4. **Assyrian archivists recorded what event in 763 B.C. which was also recorded in Amos 8:9?**
   A. the eclipse of the moon
   B. the emperor's death
   C. The Beatles *White* Album
   D. the eclipse of the sun

5. **Abraham was born in what millenium B.C.?**
   - **A.** 1st
   - **B.** 2nd
   - **C.** 3rd
   - **D.** 4th

6. **Abraham died in what millenium B.C.?**
   - **A.** 1st
   - **B.** 2nd
   - **C.** 3rd
   - **D.** 4th

7. **David's reign as King was in the same century as:**
   - **A.** plague kills 50,000 in Israel
   - **B.** Columbus discovers the new world

C. first map of the world created
D. first stamped coins appear in Lydia

8. Noah's ark rested on Mt. Ararat in what year?
A. 2348 B.C.
B. 2000 B.C.
C. 2000 A.D.
D. 3521 B.C.

MATCHING

1. Abraham arrives in Canaan	a. 984 B.C.
2. Absalom's Rebellion	b. 4004 B.C.
3. Beer is invented by Egyptians	c. 2153 B.C.
4. Virgil writes the Aeneid	d. 404 B.C.
5. Moses builds the Ark of the Covenant	e. 1491 B.C.
6. Solomon worships Ashtaroth	f. 24 B.C.
7. Amalekites attack Israel	g. 1507 B.C.
8. The term "agnostic" is coined	h. 1024–1023 B.C.
9. The Aeropagus is founded	i. 1491 B.C.
10. Adam and Eve were created	j. A.D. 1876

ANSWERS p. 284

FILL IN THE BLANKS

1. Pope Felix III instituted the holiday _____ _____ in A.D. 487.

2. Monk Dionysius Exiguus invented the term _____ in A.D. 532.

3. Jesus Christ appointed the _____ _____ in A.D. 31.

4. Paul _____ on _____ Hill in A.D. 52.

5. "_____ _____!" is the greeting the angel Gabriel gave to Mary, and was made an expression of devotion by Pope John XXI in _____ _____.

6. The _____ of John was written around A.D. 95.

7. The temple of _____ was destroyed in 884 B.C.

8. _____ reigned over Assyria in 2245 B.C.

WORD BANK

A.D.	Genesis	Revelation
B.C.	Easter Sunday	Nimrod
built a home	Summit	Ash Wednesday
Baal	Saul	Ave Maria
326 A.D.	50 A.D.	preached
Mars	12 disciples	

PUT THE FOLLOWING IN ORDER (from oldest to most recent)

1. King David's reign ends
2. First Olympic Competition
3. Events in the Acts of the Apostles take place
4. Bananas and tea appear in India
5. Ammonites attack Israel
6. Jerusalem destroyed by Sennacherib's army
7. Muhammed announces himself the "Messenger of God" and founds Islam
8. Prophets Amos and Hosea are active
9. Baal is worshipped by King Ahab
10. Jesus Christ is born

ANSWERS p. 286

TRUE OR FALSE

1. The period of the Judges lasted from 1375 to 1050 B.C.
2. Ehud was a judge for only 3 years.
3. Esther ruled as a queen in the fifth century B.C.
4. The temple was destroyed in Jerusalem around 608 B.C.
5. Around 1444 B.C. the Tabernacle was built by divinely appointed artisans.
6. Prince wanted to party like it was 1999.
7. The Romans destroyed Herod's Temple shortly before Christ's death.
8. Paul was converted almost a decade after Christ's death.
9. Paul's first missionary journey was almost ten to fifteen years after his conversion.

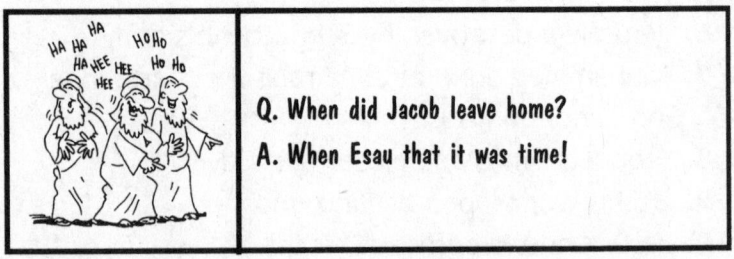

Q. When did Jacob leave home?

A. When Esau that it was time!

10. Paul was in his fifties when he went on his missionary journeys and was almost in his eighties when he died.

SHORT ANSWER

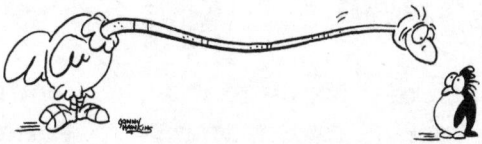

1. The tower of Babel, built c. 2247 B.C., was an event that occurred before or after Noah and the Flood?

_____

2. What did the Egyptians not wear that the Assyrians did, and, in 1490 B.C. the Jews were forbidden to mar? _____

3. What was built in Bethlehem in A.D. 325 at the supposed site of Christ's birth? _____

4. During which century did Japan and Russia each achieve translations of the Bible into their languages? _____

5. Abraham settled Canaan in 1921 B.C.; Joshua divided it when? _____

6. Canonization of martyrs and pious men as saints began when? _____

7. Childermas Day, celebrated December 28th, celebrates what? _____

MATCHING

Month of the Year	Name of the Jewish Month	Modern Equivalent
1st	Shebat	January-February
2nd	Tishri	June-July
3rd	Iyar	November-December
4th	Tammuz	April-May
5th	Chislev	September-October
6th	Adar	July-August
7th	Nisan	February-March
8th	Elul	May-June
9th	Heshvan	March-April
10th	Tebeth	October-November
11th	Ab	December-January
12th	Sivan	August-September

MULTIPLE CHOICE

1. **Elijah and Elisha lived when in relation to King David:**
   A. 100 years before him
   B. 100 years after him

C. at the same time as him
D. 200 years before him

2. **Around 773 B.C., Micah and Isaiah warned Israel that this nation would be an instrument of God's displeasure against them:**
   A. Babylon
   B. Rhythm Nation
   C. Egypt
   D. Assyria

ANSWERS p. 289

3. **The most common animal sacrifice among Indian kingdoms around 600 B.C. was:**
   A. horse
   B. dove

C. hermit crab
D. lamb

4. **The Book of Daniel, written c. 165 B.C., tells of events that happened during his Babylonian captivity:**
   A. 100 years earlier
   B. 1,000 years earlier
   C. 50 years later
   D. 400 years earlier

HOW ABOUT THAT!

The day of the year on the Jewish calendar on which Jesus rose from the dead is the same day of the year that the ark came to rest on Mt. Ararat.

5. **First and Second Chronicles were completed about the same time as what major event?**
   A. Muhammed's vision
   B. Buddha's vision
   C. Pearlvision
   D. The formation of India as a nation

6. **Ezra, who led Jews back to Jerusalem in 458 B.C., had what job title?**

A. Babylonian magician
B. Babylonian priest and scribe
C. Israelite prophet and leader
D. Israelite priest

7. **Who destroyed the Jewish temple of Jehovah on the River Nile in 410 B.C.?**
   A. Israelite loyalists
   B. aliens from the planet Nebali
   C. Assyrian rebels
   D. Egyptian priests

8. **Simon Maccabaeus, hero of the apocryphal book bearing his name, established his Hasmonaean dynasty when?**
   A. 142–135 B.C.
   B. 521–490 B.C.
   C. 8/7 Central
   D. A.D. 200–300

FILL IN THE BLANKS

1. Dionysus, who was honored by a frieze in Pompeii in _____ B.C., was the _____ god of _____.

2. Jesus Christ was probably born in the year _____ _____.

3. _____ _____ _____, major religious figure, was beheaded by King Herod in A.D. 27.

4. Saul of Tarsus became _____ on the road to _____ in A.D. 33.

5. The apostle Thomas was martyred in _____ in A.D. 50.

6. _____, a major religion in Britain, ends in A.D. 61, with the Roman conquest of Britain.

7. The community of Qumran was destroyed in A.D. 73, but they left behind the _____ _____ _____.

8. Followers of Christ were first called _____ in the year A.D. _____.

WORD BANK

100 A.D.	John the Baptist	Paul
India	the Apocrypha	German
wine	Russia	4 B.C.	Druidism
Dead Sea Scrolls	Damascus	Greek

Top Ten Events in Bible History Not Recorded in the Bible

10. Moses parts his hair

9. Peter walks in the bathtub water

8. Balaam's donkey meets Mr. Ed

7. Peter cuts off the ear of corn

6. Joseph receives his sock of many colors

5. Methusaleh's bungee-jumping tragedy

4. Solomon locks himself in a closet

3. Daniel is thrown into the lion's living room

2. Noah treats his family to a steak dinner on the ark

1. David empties his water pistol on Goliath

PUT THE FOLLOWING IN ORDER (from longest life to shortest life)

1. Noah
2. Adam
3. Abraham
4. Isaac
5. Enoch
6. Seth
7. Joseph
8. Methuselah
9. Lamech
10. Jacob

ANSWERS p. 290

TRUE OR FALSE

1. *Genesis* covers approximately 3,000 years of history.

2. *Numbers* contains events that happened in the course of 1 year.

3. Siddhartha Guatama, a.k.a. Buddha, was a contemporary of Isaiah.

4. The Jews, under leadership of Simeon Bar-Kokhba, launched an attack against the Romans which they won in 135 B.C.

5. St. Denis converted Paris to Christianity in A.D. 500.

6. In A.D. 325, a major council was held by the Emperor Constantine to discuss the canon.

7. The word "God" does not appear in the book of Esther.

8. St. Patrick of Ireland chronologically comes before the Emperor Justinian.

9. St. Columba reportedly saw the Loch Ness Monster about the same time as Buddhism became the state religion of Japan.

10. Buddhism was declared the state religion of China in A.D. 300, almost 1,000 years after it was introduced (and the same year that St. Jerome began his work on the Vulgate Bible).

MULTIPLE CHOICE (on 20th-century dates)

1. **In 1908, Pope Pius X declared what about the United States of America?**
   - **A.** It was a center of religious revival.
   - **B.** U.S. Citizens could be canonized.
   - **C.** It was no longer a missionary area.
   - **D.** The Vatican was moving to Iowa.

2. **Billy Graham, born in North Carolina in 1918, was born the same year as:**

A. James Dean and Greta Garbo
B. Elvis
C. Ella Fitzgerald and Nelson Mandela
D. Margaret Thatcher and Bob Dylan

3. In 1922 the U.S. Episcopal Church deleted what word from the traditional marriage vows:
A. submit
B. honor
C. love
D. obey

4. In what year did Mother Teresa begin her ministry in Calcutta:
A. 1948
B. 1909
C. 1960
D. 1808

5. Leaders of the World Christian Church celebrated what in Moscow in 1988?
A. the end of communist control
B. 1,000 years of Christianity in Russia
C. the entrance of Christianity to Russia
D. the opening of Moscow McDonald's (over 1 billion served)

6. What was the center of attention at a controversial auction on June 26, 1984?
A. a piece of Noah's ark
B. a scrap torn from the Shroud of Turin

C. a Faberge egg
D. 32 Hebrew manuscripts

7. **In October 1979, Pope John Paul II made the first papal visit to what country:**
   A. Afghanistan
   B. Ireland
   C. Italy
   D. Russia

ANSWERS p. 291

8. **November 26, 1976 marked what change in Italy?**
   A. There was no more spaghetti.
   B. A new pope was installed.
   C. Catholicism was no longer the state religion.
   D. Structural additions were made to the Vatican.

ANSWERS TO: WHEN?

The information found in this chapter is found in the books:

Mellersh, H. E. L. *Chronology of World History.* 4 vols. Santa Barbara, CA: Helicon Publishers, 1999.

Vincent, Benjamin. *Haydn's Dictionary of Dates.* New York: G. P. Putnam's Sons, 1894.

MULTIPLE CHOICE

#	ANSWER
1.	c
2.	a
3.	b
4.	d
5.	c
6.	b
7.	c
8.	a

MATCHING

#	ANSWER
1.	c
2.	h

#	ANSWER
3.	d
4.	f
5.	i
6.	a
7.	e
8.	j
9.	g
10.	b

FILL IN THE BLANKS

#	ANSWER
1.	Ash Wednesday
2.	A.D.
3.	twelve disciples
4.	preached, Mars
5.	Ave Maria, 326 A.D.
6.	Revelation
7.	Baal
8.	Nimrod

PUT THE FOLLOWING IN ORDER

#	ANSWER	DATE
1.	Bananas and tea appear in India	2000 B.C.
2.	Ammorites attack Israel	1143 B.C.
3.	King David's reign ends	961 B.C.
4.	Baal is worshipped by King Ahab	918 B.C.
5.	First Olympic Competition	776 B.C.
6.	Prophets Amos and Hosea are active	765–735 B.C.
7.	Jerusalem is destroyed by Sennacherib's army	700 B.C.
8.	Jesus Christ is born	4 B.C.
9.	Events in the Acts of the Apostles take place	63 A.D.
10.	Muhammed announces himself the "Messenger of God" and founds Islam	610 A.D.

Q. What was Boaz's condition before he met Naomi's daughter-in-law?

A. He was Ruth-less!

TRUE OR FALSE

#	ANSWER	REFERENCE
1.	True	
2.	False; 80	Judges 3:30
3.	True	
4.	True	
5.	True	
6.	True	
7.	False; 70 A.D.	
8.	False; 34–35 A.D.	Acts 9:1–19
9.	True	
10.	False; died at age 60–70	Acts 28

SHORT ANSWER

#	ANSWER
1.	before
2.	beards
3.	a convent
4.	19th century

SHORT ANSWER—cont'd

#	ANSWER
5.	1445 B.C.
6.	A.D. 800
7.	the memory of the Holy Innocents

MATCHING

#	ANSWER
1st	Nisan—March-April
2nd	Iyar—April-May
3rd	Sivan—May-June
4th	Tammuz—June-July
5th	Ab—July-August
6th	Elul—August-September
7th	Tishri—September-October
8th	Heshvan—October-November
9th	Chislev—November-December
10th	Tebeth—December-January
11th	Shebat—January-February
12th	Adar—February-March

MULTIPLE CHOICE

#	ANSWER
1.	b
2.	d
3.	a
4.	d
5.	b
6.	b
7.	d
8.	a

FILL IN THE BLANKS

#	ANSWER
1.	50 B.C., Greek, wine
2.	4 B.C.
3.	John the Baptist
4.	Paul, Damascus
5.	India
6.	Druidism
7.	Dead Sea Scrolls
8.	Christians, 47 A.D.

PUT THE FOLLOWING IN ORDER

#	ANSWER	AGE
1.	Methuselah	969 years
2.	Noah	950 years
3.	Adam	930 years
4.	Seth	912 years
5.	Lamech	777 years
6.	Enoch	365 years
7.	Isaac	180 years
8.	Abraham	175 years
9.	Jacob	147 years
10.	Joseph	110 years

TRUE OR FALSE

#	ANSWER
1.	True
2.	True
3.	True
4.	False; lost the battle

TRUE OR FALSE

#	ANSWER
5.	False; A.D. 275
6.	True
7.	True
8.	True
9.	True
10.	False; 350 years later

MULTIPLE CHOICE

#	ANSWER
1.	c
2.	c
3.	d
4.	a
5.	b
6.	d
7.	b
8.	c

WHEN THE BOOKS WERE WRITTEN (OR COMPILED)

OLD TESTAMENT IN CANONICAL ORDER

Genesis	ca. 1400 B.C.
Exodus	ca. 1400 B.C.
Leviticus	ca. 1400 B.C.
Numbers	ca. 1400 B.C.
Deuteronomy	ca. 1400 B.C.
Joshua	1235 B.C.
Judges	1025 B.C.
Ruth	990 B.C.
1 Samuel	1000–850 B.C.
2 Samuel	1000–850 B.C.
1 Kings	970–850 B.C.
2 Kings	850–586 B.C.
1 Chronicles	350 B.C.
2 Chronicles	350 B.C.
Ezra	445 B.C.
Nehemiah	445 B.C.
Esther	486–465 B.C.
Job	ca. 900 B.C.
Psalms	970–500 B.C.
Proverbs	ca. 900 B.C.
Ecclesiastes	962–922 B.C.
Song of Solomon	962–922 B.C.
Isaiah	700–680 B.C.
Jeremiah	585 B.C.
Lamentations	585 B.C.
Ezekiel	593–571 B.C.
Daniel	605–530 B.C.

Hosea	755–715 B.C.
Joel	835–796 B.C.
Amos	765–750 B.C.
Obadiah	848–841 B.C.
Jonah	780–750 B.C.
Micah	700–690 B.C.
Nahum	630–612 B.C.
Habakkuk	625 B.C.
Zephaniah	ca. 621 B.C.
Haggai	520 B.C.
Zechariah	520–515 B.C.
Zechariah (after chapters 9–14)	after 500 B.C.
Malachi	450 B.C.

OLD TESTAMENT IN CHRONOLOGICAL ORDER

Genesis	ca. 1400 B.C.
Exodus	ca. 1400 B.C.
Leviticus	ca. 1400 B.C.
Numbers	ca. 1400 B.C.
Deuteronomy	ca. 1400 B.C.
Joshua	1235 B.C.
Judges	1025 B.C.
1 Samuel	1000–850 B.C.
2 Samuel	1000–850 B.C.
Ruth	990 B.C.
1 Kings	970–850 B.C.
Psalms	970–500 B.C.
Ecclesiastes	962–922 B.C.
Song of Solomon	962–922 B.C.
Job	ca. 900 B.C.

Proverbs	ca. 900 B.C.
2 Kings	850–586 B.C.
Obadiah	848–841 B.C.
Joel	835–796 B.C.
Jonah	780–750 B.C.
Amos	765–750 B.C.
Hosea	755–715 B.C.
Micah	700–690 B.C.
Isaiah	700–680 B.C.
Nahum	630–612 B.C.
Zephaniah	ca. 621 B.C.
Habakkuk	625 B.C.
Daniel	605–530 B.C.
Ezekiel	593–571 B.C.
Jeremiah	585 B.C.
Lamentations	585 B.C.
Haggai	520 B.C.
Zechariah	520–515 B.C.
Zechariah (after chapters 9–14)	after 500 B.C.
Esther	486–465 B.C.
Malachi	450 B.C.
Ezra	445 B.C.
Nehemiah	445 B.C.
1 Chronicles	350 B.C.
2 Chronicles	350 B.C.

NEW TESTAMENT IN CANONICAL ORDER

Matthew	A.D. 75
Mark	A.D. 60s
Luke	A.D. 58–63
John	A.D. 90–100

Acts	A.D. 63
Romans	A.D. 56–58
1 Corinthians	A.D. 54–55
2 Corinthians	A.D. 55–56
Galatians	A.D. 55–56
Ephesians	A.D. 61–62
Philippians	A.D. 61–62
Colossians	A.D. 62–63
1 Thessalonians	A.D. 51–52
2 Thessalonians	A.D. 51–52
1 Timothy	A.D. 64
2 Timothy	A.D. 64
Titus	A.D. 64
Philemon	A.D. 62
Hebrews	A.D. 68
James	A.D. 45
1 Peter	A.D. 64
2 Peter	A.D. 66
1 John	A.D. 85–90
2 John	A.D. 96
3 John	A.D. 97
Jude	A.D. 90
Revelation	A.D. 96

NEW TESTAMENT IN CHRONOLOGICAL ORDER

James	A.D. 45
1 Thessalonians	A.D. 51–52
2 Thessalonians	A.D. 51–52
1 Corinthians	A.D. 54–55
2 Corinthians	A.D. 55–56

Galatians	A.D. 55–56
Luke	A.D. 58–63
Romans	A.D. 56–58
Mark	A.D. 60s
Ephesians	A.D. 61–62
Philippians	A.D. 61–62
Philemon	A.D. 62
Colossians	A.D. 62–63
Acts	A.D. 63
1 Timothy	A.D. 64
2 Timothy	A.D. 64
Titus	A.D. 64
1 Peter	A.D. 64
2 Peter	A.D. 66
Hebrews	A.D. 68
Matthew	A.D. 75
1 John	A.D. 85–90
Jude	A.D. 90
John	A.D. 90–100
2 John	A.D. 96
Revelation	A.D. 96
3 John	A.D. 97

Where in the World?

MULTIPLE CHOICE

1. **Eden was watered by what?**
   - **A.** rain
   - **B.** a river
   - **C.** Adam and Eve
   - **D.** angels

ANSWERS p. 312

2. **Where did the ark rest after the flood?**
   - **A.** Mt. Ararat
   - **B.** Mt. Olives
   - **C.** Mt. Horeb
   - **D.** Mt. Rushmore

HOW ABOUT THAT!

Psalm 117 is the exact middle of the Bible and also the shortest chapter in the Bible, with only two verses!

3. **What name did Jacob give the place where he dreamed about a ladder reaching to heaven?**
   - **A.** Luz
   - **B.** Bethel

C. Bed
D. Gerar

4. **Moses fled to which city after he killed the Egyptian?**
   A. Canaan
   B. Edom
   C. Midian
   D. Carson City

MATCHING

Place	Event
1. Ur	a. Job's homeland
2. Sodom and Gomorrah	b. 10 Commandments given
3. Jericho	c. Alice falls in hole
4. Moab	d. Abram's early life
5. Uz	e. Rahab lives and helps spies
6. Shushan	f. Saul's disobedient sacrifice
7. Wonderland	g. Tower of Babel
8. Gilgal	h. Esther becomes Queen
9. Mt. Sinai	i. Moses died
10. Shinar	j. God destroyed them

PUT THE FOLLOWING IN ORDER (where they lived, from birth to death)

Abraham:

1. Ur
2. Mamre
3. Mt. Moriah
4. Shechem
5. Haran
6. Bethel

ANSWERS p. 313

Jacob:

1. Bethel
2. Penuel

3. Haran
4. Mamre
5. Beersheba
6. Egypt

UNSCRAMBLE

1. Deen
2. Oirjech
3. Doosm
4. Ru

5. Resial
6. Ybonlab
7. Zaratneh
8. More
9. Wen Kory Tyci
10. Nitorch

ANSWERS p. 314

FILL IN THE BLANKS

1. Joseph took his family to _____ so that Herod could not kill Jesus.

2. _____ was the king of Judah when Jesus was born in Jerusalem.

3. "You, _____, who are exalted to heaven, will be brought down to Hades," was _____'s prediction about the city.

4. Jesus told Peter that He would give him the keys to _____.

5. Jesus arranged to meet his disciples at _____ after his resurrection.

WORD BANK

Heaven	Judea	Capernaum
Herod	Galilee	Egypt

TALL TALE

When the disciples were _____ (VERB (-ING)) through the city of _____ (CITY), they came upon a _____ (NOUN) who claimed to have met a famous rabbi. They asked him, "_____ (QUESTION)," to which he replied that he did not know. They _____ (VERB (PAST TENSE)) him, "Then how do you know you met him?" Because he was _____ (VERB (-ING)) the _____ (NOUNS) and talking to the little children. The _____ (ADJECTIVE) disciples were confused by this explanation. How could this _____ (NOUN) think that _____ (PRONOUN) _____ (VERB) who this rabbi is? Have

Top Ten Commandments Not Given on Mt. Sinai

10. Humor thy father and mother.

9. Thou shalt not mumble.

8. Thou shalt not remove thy mattress tags.

7. Remember thy Swiss cheese and keep it holy.

6. Remember thy shower and use it daily.

5. Thou shalt not toilet paper thy neighbor's house.

4. Thou shalt take thy IV in vein.

3. Try not to steal.

2. Thou shalt not covet thy neighbor's riding lawnmower.

1. Remember the Alamo.

they seen him in the _____ (PRINT MATERIAL)?

Surely not. After they _____ (VERB) and

_____ (VERB), they came to the conclusion that the _____ (NOUN) was right because, _____ (EXCUSE)!

TRUE OR FALSE

1. Jesus came from Nazareth to the Jordan to be baptized by John the Baptist.
2. Jesus was tempted on the Mount of Olives.
3. Simon and James had were from Bethsaida but had houses in Capernaum.
4. John the Baptist's family lived in the hill country of Judah.
5. Nazareth was known as "The city of David."

Q. Which area of Palestine was particularly wealthy?

A. The area around the Jordan because the banks were always overflowing.

6. Capernaum was the home base of Jesus' travels during his ministry.

7. Jesus cleansed the temple during Passover in Bethlehem.

8. Jesus was in Galilee, near the sea, when the Jews took up stones to kill him for blasphemy.

9. The Jews led Jesus from Caiaphas to the Praetorium, but would not go inside so that they would not be defiled.

10. The apostles were in Jerusalem when Jesus told them to wait for the Promise of the Father.

MULTIPLE CHOICE

1. **Before his ascension, Jesus told the disciples to be witnesses to:**
   A. Jerusalem
   B. Judea and Samaria
   C. the ends of the earth
   D. all of the above

ANSWERS p. 315

2. **Where did the disciples gather to wait for the gift of the Holy Spirit?**
   A. the temple
   B. an upper room
   C. Mt. Olivet
   D. Godot

3. **What is the name of the porch on the temple?**
   A. the outer court
   B. Solomon's porch
   C. the son room
   D. David's porch

4. **The road from Jerusalem to Gaza travels through which kind of terrain?**
   A. desert
   B. countryside
   C. mountains
   D. virtual reality

MATCHING

Place	Event
1. Damascus	a. Disciples first called Christians
2. Corinth	b. Name means "little fountains"
3. Antioch	c. Phoebe delivers Paul's letter to this church
4. Galatia	d. Believer's turn to a different gospel
5. Ephesus	e. Converts include pagan idolaters, God-fearing Greeks, and Jews

Place	**Event**
6. Philippi	f. Paul preaches first sermon
7. Thessalonica	g. Philemon's hometown
8. Colosse	h. Center for pagan worship and magical arts
9. Rome	i. John writes Revelation here
10. Patmos	j. Chloe's church is here

PUT THE FOLLOWING IN ORDER

(Paul's first missionary journey from start to finish)

1. Antioch
2. Pisidian Antioch
3. Derbe
4. Seleucia
5. Paphos
6. Perga
7. Attalia
8. Iconium
9. Lystra
10. Salamis

(some will be used twice)

ANSWERS p. 316

MULTIPLE CHOICE (some have more than one answer)

1. **Which of the following were churches addressed in Revelation?**
   - **A.** Pergamos
   - **B.** Thyatira
   - **C.** Sardis
   - **D.** First Presbyterian
   - **E.** Philadelphia
   - **F.** All of the above

2. **In the throne room of Heaven there are which of the following:**
   - **A.** a rainbow
   - **B.** an emerald throne
   - **C.** twenty-four thrones
   - **D.** lightning and thunder
   - **E.** lamps of fire
   - **F.** a sea of glass, like crystal
   - **G.** a McDonalds

3. **Where were the four angels standing when they opened the scrolls?**
   - **A.** the throne room
   - **B.** the four corners of the earth
   - **C.** on their heads
   - **D.** in the four churches

4. Where does the River of Life proceed from?

A. the new Euphrates
B. the tree of life
C. God's throne
D. the Lamb of God

ANSWERS p. 317

ANSWERS TO: WHERE IN THE WORLD?

MULTIPLE CHOICE

#	ANSWER	REFERENCE
1.	b	Genesis 2:10
2.	a	Genesis 8:4
3.	b	Genesis 28:19
4.	c	Exodus 2:15

MATCHING

#	ANSWER	REFERENCE
1.	d	Genesis 11
2.	j	Genesis 19
3.	e	Joshua 2
4.	i	Deuteronomy 34:5
5.	a	Job 1
6.	h	Esther 1:1
7.	c	Alice's Adventures in Wonderland
8.	f	2 Samuel 2:4
9.	b	Exodus 19
10.	g	Genesis 11

PUT THE FOLLOWING IN ORDER

# ANSWER	REFERENCE
Abraham:	
1. Ur; birthplace	
2. Haran; dwells with father, nephew Lot, and wife Sarai	
3. Shechem; builds altar at terebinth tree of Moreh	Genesis 12:6,7
4. Bethel; builds altar at the mountain east of Bethel	Genesis 12:8
5. Mt. Moriah; Abraham takes Isaac to be sacrificed	Genesis 22
6. Mamre; buried	Genesis 25
Jacob:	
1. Beersheba; birthplace	Genesis 25:24–34
2. Bethel; dreams of angels going up and down staircase to heaven	Genesis 28:1–19
3. Haran; marries Leah and Rachel	Genesis 29:15–28
4. Penuel; wrestles with an angel	Genesis 32:22–32
5. Egypt; travels to escape famine with 12 sons	Genesis 46:1–6
6. Mamre; buried	Genesis 50:13–14

UNSCRAMBLE

#	ANSWER
1.	Eden
2.	Jericho
3.	Sodom
4.	Ur
5.	Israel
6.	Babylon
7.	Nazareth
8.	Rome
9.	New York City
10.	Corinth

FILL IN THE BLANKS

#	ANSWER	REFERENCE
1.	Egypt	Matthew 2:14
2.	Herod	Matthew 2:1
3.	Capernaum, Jesus	Matthew 11:23
4.	Heaven	Matthew 16:18–19
5.	Galilee	Matthew 20:10

TRUE OR FALSE

#	ANSWER	REFERENCE
1.	True	Mark 1:9
2.	False	Mark 1:12–13
3.	False	John 1:44
4.	True	Luke 1:39–66
5.	False	Luke 2:4
6.	True	Luke 4:31
7.	False	John 2:13–16
8.	False	John 10:23, 31
9.	True	John 18:28
10.	True	Acts 1:4

MULTIPLE CHOICE

#	ANSWER	REFERENCE
1.	d	Acts 1:8
2.	b	Acts 1:13
3.	b	Acts 3:11
4.	a	Acts 8:26

MATCHING

#	ANSWER	REFERENCE
1.	f	Acts 9:19–20
2.	j	1 Corinthians 1:11
3.	a	Acts 11:26
4.	d	Galatians 1:6
5.	h	Acts 19:35
6.	b	from the Greek, Krenides
7.	e	1 Thessalonians 1:8, 10; 17:4
8.	g	Colossians 4:7–9
9.	c	Romans 16:1
10.	i	Revelation 1:9

PUT THE FOLLOWING IN ORDER

#	ANSWER	REFERENCE
1.	Antioch (In Syria)	Acts 13
2.	Seleucia (In Syria)	Acts 13
3.	Salamis (In Cyprus)	Acts 13
4.	Paphos (In Cyprus)	Acts 13
5.	Perga (Mediterranean Coast)	Acts 13
6.	Pisidian Antioch (In Phrygia)	Acts 13

#	ANSWER	REFERENCE
7.	Iconium (In Lycaonia)	Acts 14
8.	Lystra (In Lycaonia)	Acts 14
9.	Derbe (In Lycaonia)	Acts 14
10.	Back to Lystra	
11.	Back to Iconium	
12.	Back to Pisidian Antioch	
13.	Back to Perga	
14.	To Attalia	
15.	Back to Seleucia	
16.	Back to Antioch	

MULTIPLE CHOICE

#	ANSWER	REFERENCE
1.	a,b,c,e	Revelation 2–3
2.	a,b,c,d,e,f	Revelation 4
3.	b	Revelation 7
4.	c	Revelation 22

Women's Issues

MULTIPLE CHOICE

1. **According to the Genesis Story, Eve's function was:**
   - **A.** Adam's helper
   - **B.** $e=mc^2$
   - **C.** to watch over the animals
   - **D.** gardener

ANSWERS p. 339

HOW ABOUT THAT!

The Book of Esther, like Song of Solomon, doesn't ever mention the name of God!

2. **More space is devoted to this woman than any other in the Bible:**
   - **A.** Eve
   - **B.** Sarah
   - **C.** Esther
   - **D.** Whoopi

3. **Who is the only wife named among the "heroes of the faith"?**

A. Sarah
B. Ruth
C. Wilma
D. Esther

4. **Hagar was the mother of:**
   A. Mephibosheth
   B. Jacob
   C. Yanni
   D. Ishmael

TRUE OR FALSE

1. Lot's wife's name is never mentioned.
2. Rebekah was Jacob's bride.
3. Rebekah's choice to marry and leave home was her own.
4. Rachel gave birth to Jacob's favorite son.
5. Leah had "delicate" or "weak" eyes.

Q. Who was the largest woman in the Bible?
A. The woman of Some Area!

6. Dinah was one of Jacob's two daughters.

7. Tamar disguised herself as a fortune-teller in order to trick her father-in-law into sleeping with her.

8. Moses sent his wife Zipporah back to live at her father's house.

ANSWERS p. 339

9. Moses married an Ethopian woman.

10. Miriam was struck with leprosy after criticizing Moses' choice of a wife.

FILL IN THE BLANKS

1. Rebekah favored _____ over _____.

2. Rachel was _____ _____ when she first met Jacob.

3. Dinah was _____ by the prince of Shechem.

ANSWERS p. 340

4. _____ was Moses' mother.

5. Miriam, Moses' sister, was gifted as a _____ and _____.

WORD BANK

tending sheep | musician | Jacob
prophetess | Esau | Jochebed
making pots

HOW ABOUT THAT!

God changed Jacob's name to Israel because he was a fighter, one who prevailed.

WORD SEARCH

Lot's Wife	Elizabeth	Martha
Tamar	Jezebel	Dorcus
Lydia	Sapphira	Naomi
The Servant Girl	Abigail	Orpha
Rebekah	The Virgin Mary	Delilah
Miriam	Mary Magdalene	Rahab
Dinah	Hannah	Eve

N I N Y E M L Q U P T U B M F H K O D A
J K A C U E N O G S A B O L X S I J R W
P I L R S T I U W K M N E H Y C U D S T
K M O F G U T R K I A V B T W D F A D S
T E T P U T H E S E R V A N T G I R L O
O U S T E X W B N Y I L J D E H M A W R
O M W L I T E E V U T J D A F K Y E X B
L O I B E S N K G R S J T I B N G D S O
O L F R N K G A D Y K N D O P I D R E G
K P E D I N A H N G J F E Y H R G S R E
L N F S G A J O R U E J C D S H K A L I
P O L H Y E M E L I Z A B E T H I P I Q
T P O B D H K Y P N E N R U T B E P U L
H O P E C I T Y U N B R O M A N C H E I
E N H G T H E S T O E N E D T O D I D A
V M A R Y M A G D A L E N E N R D R K A
I T N E E T U E A N U R M L E A G A E T
R T N I N G H I M A T C E I R H R I E D
G O A N A U G T H I U S T L E A N T E T
I U H K L M N E C O R P H A L B E O P A
N T R A V A A N M U R I T H O R I A N C
M A N D O R C U S O N P A T R I A T I O
A P N U G T A S T N Y K E P A T K I N L
R R O C K H U D S O N A N V D K I M M I
Y E L A N A O M I B E L L I E O P B N R
K I O P H G D A B I O P M G E X H T J N

UNSCRAMBLE

1. Pozrahip
2. Calhre
3. Hrut dna Animo
4. Yarm Degnlamea
5. Braah
6. Thebaabsh
7. Rasha
8. Ramy dan Thamra
9. Lebezje
10. Kerbeah

ANSWERS p. 342

MATCHING

1. Mahlah, Noah, Hoglah, Milcah, and Tirzah	a. father offered her as a wife to whoever could defeat Kirjath Sepher
2. Rahab	b. name means "bee"
3. Achsah	c. cut Samson's hair
4. Deborah	d. Boaz was one of her offspring
5. Jael	e. warned by an angel that she would have a child
6. Samson's mother	f. her son stole 1000 pieces of silver from her

7. Delilah — g. free to choose husbands and inherit land

8. Micah's mother — h. raped as retribution for the Levite's concubine's death

9. daughters of Benjaminites — i. killed Sisera

10. Orpah — j. Naomi's other daughter-in-law

HOW ABOUT THAT!

Women helped Nehemiah rebuild the wall around Jerusalem! (Neh. 3:12)

MULTIPLE CHOICE

1. Ruth's name means:

A. sight, friendship
B. honor, loyalty
C. God's child
D. great baseball player

2. **Hannah was accused of what when she prayed for a child:**
   A. witchcraft
   B. grand-theft auto
   C. drunkenness
   D. laziness

ANSWERS p. 343

3. **Michal was what relation to Saul?**
   A. wife
   B. daughter
   C. sister
   D. none

4. **What happened to Michal when she made fun of King David's dancing?**

Top Ten Ways Delilah Tried to Take Away Samson's Strength Before Cutting His Hair

10. Nag, nag, nag

9. Braided his nose hairs into seven braids

8. Made him watch sappy movies

7. Threw away his old college T-shirts

6. Only fixed left-overs

5. Spent an hour each morning primping

4. Decorated the tent in pastels

3. Criticized his driving

2. Constantly reminded him of unfinished to-do lists

1. Nair

A. lost her voice
B. lost her sheep
C. lost her vision
D. lost her ability to have children

5. **Abigail, the wife of Nabal, was described as being:**
A. beautiful
B. intelligent
C. bald
D. wise with money

6. **What person did Saul approach when he wanted to know whether or not he would remain King?**
A. the fortune-teller from Barnum and Bailey
B. the palm-reader from Shechem
C. the tarot-card reader from Bezel
D. the medium of En Dor

7. **How did God come to the aid of Deborah, the judge?**
A. He sent a flood to destroy the enemy.
B. He struck the people down with a mighty gavel.
C. He sent a violent thunderstorm.
D. He sent an earthquake.

8. **Abimelech's killer was:**
A. a demon-possessed pig
B. a woman
C. a child
D. cigarettes

FILL IN THE BLANKS

1. Samson's pagan wife got her way with _____ and _____.

2. Mephibosheth was _____'s son, through his concubine _____.

3. Bathsheba was the wife of _____, the _____.

4. _____ was the mother of Solomon.

5. The _____ _____ _____ brought gifts to Solomon and praised his God.

ANSWERS p. 344

WORD BANK

Saul	Uriah	Bathsheba
Queen of Sheba	tears	Queen Latifa
Hittite	Amalekite	cooking
cleaning	whining	Rizpah

TRUE OR FALSE

1. Bathsheba mourned the death of her husband, Uriah.

2. Tamar was the daughter of King David and Princess Maacah.

3. The wise woman of Tekoa lied to King David, influencing him to forgive Amnon for raping his daughter, Tamar.

4. Jesus used the Queen of Sheba as an example when he rebuked the Pharisees.

5. All of Solomon's wives worshiped Yahweh.

6. Queen Jezebel provided a place of refuge for the prophet Elijah.

7. King Ahaz killed a man in order to usurp his vineyard.

8. The Shunammite woman and her husband built a lodging for Elisha in their home.

9. Naaman's maidservant helped her master, despite the fact that he had her stolen from her family in Israel.

10. Huldah was the prophetess to King Josiah and lived at the same time as Jeremiah and Zephaniah.

SHORT ANSWER

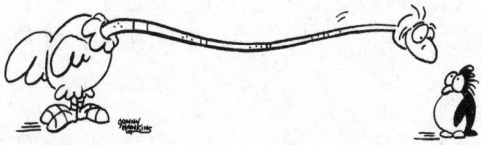

1. Elijah provided constant bread and oil for whom?

_____

_____

2. Jezebel worshipped which god? _____

_____

3. What prophecy was fulfilled when Queen Jezebel died? _____

_____

4. The widow came to Elisha for advice when what threat appeared? _____

_____

5. Elisha blessed the Shunammite woman with what?

_____

MATCHING

1. Queen Abijah	a. Mother of King Manasseh of Judah
2. Queen Athaliah	b. Mother of King Amaziah of Judah
3. Queen Azubah	c. Daughter of Zechariah; Mother of King Hezekiah of Judah
4. Queen Bathsheba	d. Wife of King Ahasuerus of Persia
5. Queen Esther	e. Mother of King Azariah of Judah

6. Queen Hamutal — f. Daughter of Jezebel and Ahab

7. Queen Hephzibah — g. Mother of King Josiah of Judah

8. Queen Jecholiah — h. Mother of King Jehoshaphat of Judah

9. Queen Jedidah — i. Daughter of Jeremiah of Libnah

10. Queen Jehoaddan — j. Mother of King Solomon

MULTIPLE CHOICE

1. **Hosea's wife Gomer was a:**
   - **A.** prophetess
   - **B.** prostitute
   - **C.** mechanic in Mayberry
   - **D.** soldier

ANSWERS p. 346

2. **The greedy women of Samaria were referred to by Amos as:**
   - **A.** harlots of Samaria
   - **B.** penny-pinchers of Ashur
   - **C.** cows of Bashan
   - **D.** curs of Bashan

3. **Zechariah had a vision of what as a representation of evil:**
   A. a woman in a basket
   B. a female dog eating raw meat
   C. Dr. Evil, Austin Powers' nemesis
   D. a woman speaking in tongues

4. **Ninevah was called what for enticing other nations?**
   A. bratty
   B. deceptive
   C. a magician
   D. a harlot

FILL IN THE BLANKS

1. Peter's _____-_____-_____ was healed when Jesus touched her. After she was healed, she arose and _____ _____ _____.

2. The hemorrhaging woman was healed because of her _____ which was displayed when she _____ Jesus' _____.

3. The Canaanite woman's daughter was healed because her mother _____ _____ _____ _____.

4. The infirm woman responded to Jesus' healing by being made _____ and _____ _____.

ANSWERS p. 346

WORD BANK

Faith knowledge

straight mother-in-law

cut feet

great-great aunt

served those present

touched started singing garment

persistently showed her faith

MATCHING (Jesus in His last days)

Woman	Event	Action
1. Unnamed Woman	a. the testing of Peter	i. pleaded with her husband to release Jesus

MATCHING—cont'd

Woman	Event	Action
2. Servant Girl #1	b. the Resurrection	ii. stood by the cross, suffering with Jesus
3. Servant Girl #2	c. the Crucifixion	iii. prepared Jesus' body for burial
4. Pilate's Wife	d. the journey to the Crucifixion	iv. asked Peter about his association with Jesus
5. Unnamed Women	e. the testing of Peter	v. used expensive oil to annoint Jesus
6. The three Marys	f. the annointing of Jesus at Bethany	vi. asked Peter about his association with Jesus
7. Women from Galilee	g. the trial of Jesus	vii. mourned for Jesus
8. Mary Magdalene, Mary the mother of James, Joanna	h. the crucifixion and burial	viii. the first to announce his resurrection

ANSWERS TO: WOMEN'S ISSUES

MULTIPLE CHOICE

#	ANSWER	REFERENCE
1.	a	Genesis 2:18
2.	b	
3.	a	Hebrews 11
4.	d	Genesis 16

TRUE OR FALSE

#	ANSWER	REFERENCE
1.	True	Genesis 13–19
2.	False; Isaac	Genesis 24
3.	True	Genesis 24:57–8
4.	True	Genesis 30
5.	True	Genesis 29
6.	False; She was his only daughter.	Genesis 34
7.	False; She dressed as a prostitute.	Genesis 38

TRUE OR FALSE—cont'd

#	ANSWER	REFERENCE
8.	True	Exodus 18:2–3
9.	True	Numbers 12
10.	True	Numbers 12

FILL IN THE BLANKS

#	ANSWER	REFERENCE
1.	Jacob, Esau	Genesis 25:28
2.	tending sheep	Genesis 29
3.	raped	Genesis 34
4.	Jochebed	Exodus 2
5.	musician, prophetess	Exodus 15:20

Q. Who was the shortest man in the Old Testament?

A. Knee-high-miah!

WORD SEARCH

N I N Y E M L Q U P T U B M F H K O D A
J K A C U E N O G S A B O L X S I J R W
P I L R S T I U W K M N E H Y C U D S T
K M O F G U T R K I A V B T W D F A D S
T E T P U T H E S E R V A N T G I R L O
O U S T E X W B N Y I L J D E H M A W R
O M W L I T E E V U T J D A F K Y E X B
L O I B E S N K G R S J T I B N G D S O
O L F R N K G A D Y K N D O P I D R E G
K P E D I N A H N G J F E Y H R G S R E
L N F S G A J O R U E J C D S H K A L I
P O L H Y E M E L I Z A B E T H I P I Q
T P O B D H K Y P N E N R U T B E P U L
H O P E C I T Y U N B R O M A N C H E I
E N H G T H E S T O E N E D T O D I D A
V M A R Y M A G D A L E N E N R D R K A
I T N E E T U E A N U R M L E A G A E T
R T N I N G H I M A T C E I R H R I E D
G O A N A U G T H I U S T L E A N T E T
I U H K L M N E C O R P H A L B E O P A
N T R A V A A N M U R I T H O R I A N C
M A N D O R C U S O N P A T R I A T I O
A P N U G T A S T N Y K E P A T K I N L
R R O C K H U D S O N A N V D K I M M I
Y E L A N A O M I B E L L I E O P B N R
K I O P H G D A B I O P M G E X H T J N

UNSCRAMBLE

#	ANSWER
1.	Zipporah
2.	Rachel
3.	Ruth and Naomi
4.	Mary Magdalene
5.	Rahab
6.	Bathsheba
7.	Sarah
8.	Mary and Martha
9.	Jezebel
10.	Rebekah

MATCHING

#	ANSWER	REFERENCE
1.	g	Numbers 27
2.	d	Judges 2
3.	a	
4.	b	

#	ANSWER	REFERENCE
5.	i	Judges 5:4
6.	e	Judges 13
7.	c	Judges 16
8.	f	Judges 17
9.	h	Judges 19–20
10.	j	Ruth 1

MULTIPLE CHOICE

#	ANSWER	REFERENCE
1.	a	
2.	c	1 Samuel 1
3.	b	2 Samuel
4.	d	2 Samuel 6:23
5.	a, b	1 Samuel 25
6.	d	1 Samuel 28
7.	c	Judges 5:4
8.	b	Judges 9

FILL IN THE BLANKS

#	ANSWER	REFERENCE
1.	tears, whining	Judges 14
2.	Saul, Rizpah	2 Samuel 21
3.	Uriah, Hittite	2 Samuel 11:3
4.	Bathsheba	2 Samuel 12:24
5.	Queen of Sheba	1 Kings 10

TRUE OR FALSE

#	ANSWER	REFERENCE
1.	True	2 Samuel 11:26
2.	True	2 Samuel 3:3
3.	False; to bring Absolom back	2 Samuel 14
4.	True	Matthew 12:42
5.	False; pagan gods	Deuteronomy 4:15–20
6.	False; threatened to destroy him	1 Kings 18
7.	False; Queen Jezebel	1 Kings 21
8.	True	2 Kings 4
9.	True	2 Kings 5
10.	True	2 Kings 22

SHORT ANSWER

#	ANSWER	REFERENCE
1.	Widow of Zarephath	1 Kings 17
2.	Melquart (the Baal of Tyre)	1 Kings 18
3.	that her body would be eaten by dogs	1 Kings 21
4.	the loss of her sons	2 Kings 4
5.	fertility	2 Kings 4–8

MATCHING

#	ANSWER	REFERENCE
1.	c	2 Kings 18:2
2.	f	2 Kings 8:18, 26
3.	h	1 Kings 22:42
4.	j	2 Samuel 12:24
5.	d	Esther 2:16–17
6.	i	2 Kings 22:31
7.	a	2 Kings 21:1
8.	e	2 Kings 15:2
9.	g	2 Kings 22:1
10.	b	2 Kings 14:2

MULTIPLE CHOICE

#	ANSWER	REFERENCE
1.	b	Hosea 1–3
2.	c	Amos 4:1
3.	a	Zechariah 5:5–11
4.	d	Nahum 3:4

FILL IN THE BLANKS

#	ANSWER	REFERENCE
1.	mother-in-law, served those present	Matthew 8
2.	faith, touched, garment	Luke 8
3.	persistently showed her faith	Mark 7
4.	straight, glorifying God	Luke 13

MATCHING

#	ANSWER	REFERENCE	
1.	f	v.	Matthew 26:6–13
2.	a or e	iv. or vi.	Matthew 26:69–70

#	ANSWER	REFERENCE	
3.	e or a	vi. or iv.	Matthew 26:71–72
4.	g	i.	Matthew 27:17–19
5.	d	vii.	Luke 23:26–29
6.	c	ii.	John 19:25–27
7.	h	iii.	Matthew 27:55–56
8.	b	viii.	Matthew 28, Luke 24

When the Saints Go Marching In

MULTIPLE CHOICE

1. **St. Ambrose of Milan was elected bishop when:**
   - **A.** he healed a woman of her lifelong disease
   - **B.** he won the majority of the electoral college
   - **C.** a little boy cried out, "Ambrose, bishop!"
   - **D.** he received a revelation from God

2. **St. Ambrose dedicated himself to the eradication of:**
   - **A.** Arianism
   - **B.** Gnosticism
   - **C.** Materialism
   - **D.** Marcionism

ANSWERS p. 366

3. **On which major holiday was Ambrose buried?**
   - **A.** Christmas
   - **B.** Easter
   - **C.** Palm Sunday
   - **D.** Flag Day

4. **St. Augustine of Canterbury was called:**
   - **A.** Bob
   - **B.** Servant to the Anglo-Saxon
   - **C.** Apostle to the English
   - **D.** Disciple to the British

5. **Why was Augustine sent to England?**
   - **A.** They had received no missionaries.
   - **B.** He wanted to see the Tower of London.

C. He spoke Anglo-Saxon.
D. Pope St. Gregory the Great believed the English were as beautiful as angels.

6. **Which Augustine wrote *The Confessions of St. Augustine?***
   A. St. Augustine of Canterbury
   B. St. Augustine of Hippo
   C. St. Augustine of St. Louis
   D. St. Augustine of Rome

7. **St. Augustine of Hippo was born in which country?**
   A. Numidia (modern-day Algeria)
   B. The United States of America
   C. Italy (Rome)
   D. Crete

8. **Basil the Great had two siblings who also became:**
   A. spices
   B. missionaries
   C. saints
   D. "the Great"s

Q. How did St. Boniface get a black eye?
A. He called St. Francis a sissy.

MATCHING

1. Basil the Great	a. *Ecclesiastical History of the English People*
2. Bernard de Clairvaux	b. Franciscan monk healed by St. Francis
3. Clement of Alexandria	c. 2nd century bishop of Caesarea
4. Venerable Bede	d. patron saint of animals
5. Thomas Cranmer	e. Father of Eastern Monasticism
6. John Donne	f. attended Oxford University at age twelve
7. Bonaventure	g. brought Christianity to Armenia
8. Cornelius the Centurion	h. founded Alexandrian School of Theology
9. Francis of Assisi	i. *Book of Common Prayer*
10. Gregory the Illuminator	j. sponsored the formation of the Knights Templars—warrior monks who fought in the first Crusade

FILL IN THE BLANKS

1. Bonaventure was born in _____ and followed the teachings of St. _____.

2. Brigid of Kildare founded the first _____ _____ _____ in Ireland.

3. Clare of Assisi followed St. _____ and began a group of nuns called the _____.

4. _____ _____, while being burned at the stake, said, "As my _____ offended in writing contrary to my heart, my _____ shall first be punished," and stuck his _____ in the fire.

5. St. Etheldreda had a large swelling on her _____ that she believed was punishment for her earlier love of lavish _____.

6. St. Francis of Assisi was _____-_____ years old when he realized his calling in life.

7. St. _____ had a famous fire.

8. Ignatius of Loyola served as a boy page in the Spanish court of _____ and _____.

WORD BANK

neck Ferdinand Paul

Francis thirty-one Italy

Isabelle necklaces Elmo

Minoresses maidens hand

twenty-two Egypt

Elizabeth Thomas Cranmer

women's religious order

PUT THE FOLLOWING IN ORDER (from earliest to latest in history)

1. Venerable Bede
2. Bonaventure
3. St. Francis of Assisi
4. Hugh Latimer
5. Ignatius of Loyola
6. Irenaeus of Lyons
7. Jerome
8. Julian of Norwich
9. Justin Martyr
10. Monnica

ANSWERS p. 368

SHORT ANSWER

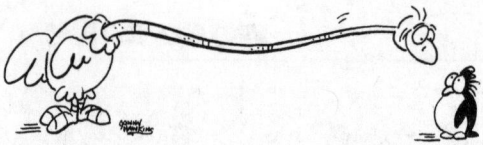

1. St. Ignatius of Loyola founded what religious society? _____

2. Irenaeus of Lyon's name appropriately means what?

_____

3. What is St. Jerome's most remembered accomplishment? _____

_____

4. John of the Cross and Teresa of Avila were co-founders of what? _____

5. Dame Julian of Norwich was one of what group of Christians? _____

6. When did the Saints last win a Super Bowl?

_____

7. How did Justin Martyr die? _____

8. Who cried out, while being burned at the stake, ". . . by God's grace we shall this day light such a candle in England as I trust shall never be put out!"? _____

UNSCRAMBLE

1. Mothas Quniaas
2. Celsausnew
3. Matsoh à Kebtec
4. Hosamt à Peksim
5. Restea fo Viaal
6. Katpicr fo Lernida
7. Teprepau
8. Lyopracp fo Mysnar
9. Sotham Remo
10. Ryneh Ymratn

ANSWERS p. 369

HOW ABOUT THAT!

In order to be a saint, a person must be able to be in direct contact with God—Pure Awareness.

MULTIPLE CHOICE

1. **St. Lucy of Sicily is symbolized by a lamp representing her pledge of:**

A. allegiance
B. virginity
C. silence
D. a chicken in the pot of every peasant

2. **Lucy's name means "light," so she was considered:**
A. a protector of the blind
B. underweight
C. a beacon
D. a judge

3. **St. Lucy's other symbol, which no one can explain the significance of, is:**
A. a mouse
B. an ostrich
C. a blind camel
D. a cat

4. **St. Margaret of Scotland brought whose reforms to the church of Scotland:**
A. John of the Cross
B. John Wycliff
C. Saint Gregory VII
D. Wyclef Jean

5. **Henry Martyn served as a chaplain for:**
A. the Notre Dame football team
B. House of Commons
C. The East India Company
D. The Royal Palace

6. **Monnica was the mother of:**
   - **A.** Pearl
   - **B.** St. Augustine of Hippo
   - **C.** St. Augustine of Canterbury
   - **D.** St. Francis of Assisi

ANSWERS p. 370

7. **Monnica's name in Greek means:**
   - **A.** One Victory
   - **B.** Peace with God
   - **C.** half of a harmonica
   - **D.** one day

8. **Thomas More is a saint in which communion:**
   - **A.** North Pole
   - **B.** Protestant

C. Catholic
D. Anglican

TRUE OR FALSE

1. St. Margaret of Scotland never married.

2. St. Patrick traveled to Ireland from Rome.

3. St. Patrick was kidnapped and sold into slavery in Ireland

4. St. Patrick used a shamrock, the three-leaved cousin to a clover, to teach the principles of the Trinity.

5. Perpetua was condemned to death at the arena and was killed by wild animals.

6. When Perpetua's executioner failed to kill her, she guided his sword toward her own death.

7. Nicholas Ridley wrote the *Book of Common Prayer.*

8. Scholastica is considered the mother of women's monasticism in the Western Church.

9. The Saint, Val Kilmer, was a man of many names.

10. Elizabeth Ann Seton was the first native-born American to be canonized as a saint.

Top Ten People Groups Still in Need of a Patron Saint

10. Parents of children with science projects due

9. The gingivitis inflicted

8. The sleep deprived

7. Internet junkies

6. Heartburn sufferers

5. The balding

4. Third-string NFL quarterbacks

3. The toothless

2. Fourth-year, undeclared-major college students

1. Chronically late employees

MATCHING

1. Swithun of Winchester	a. canonized for work with poor and orphans
2. Thomas Aquinas	b. if it rains on his feast day, then it will rain 40 more days
3. Theresa of Lisieux	c. ran away from home at age 7 to become a martyr
4. Wenceslaus	d. last words were verified: "After my death, I will let fall a shower of roses."
5. Thomas à Becket	e. Bible translator burned at the stake
6. Elizabeth Ann Seton	f. patron saint of Bohemia
7. William Tyndale	g. Murdered in the Canterbury Cathedral
8. Alban	h. wrote *Imitation of Christ*
9. Teresa of Avila	i. first British martyr
10. Thomas à Kempis	j. brilliant scholar who was called "Dumb Ox" by classmates

SHORT ANSWER

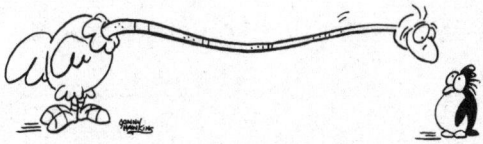

1. What was Alcuin's greatest contribution to his society? _____

_____

2. What did Ambrose do to end paganism in the Roman Empire? _____

3. What did St. Antony of Egypt never see for twenty years? _____

4. What saint was St. Benedict of Nursia's twin sister?

_____

5. St. Blaise is the patron saint of what? _____

_____

6. St. Boniface of Mainz convinced the people of the Netherlands of the power of God by doing what?

ANSWERS p. 372

_____

_____

7. St. Catherine of Siena, the youngest of twenty-five children, worked as what? _____

8. St. Cyril and St. Methodius were missionaries tc what people? _____

FILL IN THE BLANKS

1. Edward the _____ is called this because he dedicated himself to the faith, faced _____, but was not _____.

2. Fabian of Rome was elected _____ when a _____ landed on his head.

3. St. _____ is the patron saint of England.

4. _____ is revered by the _____ Church and is considered the patron saint of Russia.

WORD BANK

frightened	George	Dove
martyred	Eastern	Sergius
the mob	confessor	Pope
tailor	governor	saint

ANSWERS TO: WHEN THE SAINTS GO MARCHING IN

MULTIPLE CHOICE

#	ANSWER
1.	c
2.	a
3.	b
4.	c
5.	d
6.	b
7.	a
8.	c

MATCHING

#	ANSWER
1.	e
2.	j
3.	h
4.	a

#	ANSWER
5.	i
6.	f
7.	b
8.	c
9.	d
10.	g

FILL IN THE BLANKS

#	ANSWER
1.	Italy, Francis
2.	women's religious order
3.	Francis, Minoresses
4.	Thomas Cranmer, hand, hand, hand
5.	neck, necklaces
6.	twenty-two
7.	Elmo
8.	Ferdinand, Isabella

PUT THE FOLLOWING IN ORDER

#	ANSWER	DATE
9.	Justin Martyr	110 A.D.
6.	Irenaeus of Lyons	125 A.D.
10.	Monnica	331 A.D.
7.	Jerome	340 A.D.
1.	Venerable Bede	673 A.D.
3.	Francis of Assisi	1182 A.D.
2.	Bonaventure	1221 A.D.
8.	Julian of Norwich	1342 A.D.
4.	Hugh Latimer	1490 A.D.
5.	Ignatius of Loyola	1491 A.D.

SHORT ANSWER

#	ANSWER
1.	Jesuits
2.	Peaceful One
3.	the Vulgate Bible—translated entire Bible into Latin from Hebrew and Greek

#	ANSWER
4.	the Order of Discalced Carmelites
5.	mystics
6.	never
7.	in the arena, as a martyr
8.	Hugh Latimer

UNSCRAMBLE

#	ANSWER
1.	Thomas Aquinas
2.	Wenceslaus
3.	Thomas à Becket
4.	Thomas à Kempis
5.	Teresa of Avila
6.	Patrick of Ireland
7.	Perpetua
8.	Polycarp of Smyrna
9.	Thomas More
10.	Henry Martyn

MULTIPLE CHOICE

#	ANSWER
1.	b
2.	a
3.	d
4.	c
5.	c
6.	b
7.	a
8.	d

TRUE OR FALSE

#	ANSWER	REFERENCE
1.	False	married to a King
2.	False	born and raised in Britain
3.	True	
4.	True	
5.	False	only injured, not killed

#	ANSWER	REFERENCE
6.	True	
7.	False	helped Thomas Cranmer write it
8.	True	
9.	True	
10.	True	

MATCHING

#	ANSWER
1.	b
2.	j
3.	d
4.	f
5.	g
6.	a
7.	e
8.	i
9.	c
10.	h

SHORT ANSWER

#	ANSWER
1.	the revival of quality education, first-rate schools and universities all over Europe
2.	rallied cities against the Goths, who were destroyed
3.	a human face
4.	St. Scholastica
5.	throat diseases, because he saved a boy from choking on a fishbone
6.	chopping down a rotten tree—he was denouncing the pagan god Donar, whos symbol was the oak
7.	a nurse to lepers and cancer victims
8.	the Slavs

FILL IN THE BLANKS

#	ANSWER
1.	Confessor, death, martyred
2.	Pope, dove
3.	George
4.	Sergius, Eastern

THE INTERESTING AND UNUSUAL

1. HISTORY

It has been reported that the Bible has been the largest seller of all books published.

The Bible was written by about 40 men who engaged in writing it during a period of about 1600 years dating from 1500 B.C. to about 100 years after Christ. These men wrote as they were moved by the Holy Spirit (2 Pet. 1:21). They wrote not in words of human wisdom but in words taught by the Holy Ghost (1 Corinthians 2:13).

2. ENGLISH BIBLE

The first translation of the English Bible was initiated by John Wycliffe and completed by John Purvey in 1388.

The first American edition of the Bible was perhaps published some time before 1752.

The Bible has been translated in part or in whole (as of 1964) in over 1,200 different languages or dialects.

The Bible was divided into chapters by Stephen Langton about A.D. 1228.

The Old Testament was divided into verses by R. Nathan in A.D. 1448 and the New Testament by Robert Stephanus in A.D. 1551.

The entire Bible divided into chapters and verses first appeared in the Geneva Bible of 1560.

3. BOOKS OF THE BIBLE

Books of Bible	66
The Old Testament	39
The New Testament	27

Middle book of Old Testament ..... Proverbs
Middle book of New Testament ..... 2 Thessalonians

4. CHAPTERS OF THE BIBLE

A. Facts and figures

Entire Bible .....1189 chapters
Old Testament ..... 929 chapters
New Testament ..... 260 chapters
Middle chapter of Old Testament .....Job 29
Middle chapter of New Testament .....Romans 13
Middle and shortest chapter of the Bible.....Psalm 117
Longest chapter in the Bible .....Psalm 119
Chapters that are alike in the Bible.....2 Kings 19; Isaiah 37

B. Great Golden Chapters

Ascension .....Acts 1
Backsliders .....Hosea 14
Beatitudes .....Matthew 5,6,7
Bread of Life .....John 6
Brotherhood .....Romans 14
Builders .....Nehemiah 4
Burden-bearers .....Galatians 6
Call, Universal.....Isaiah 55
Call, Workers .....Isaiah 6
Chastening .....2 Corinthians 4
Comfort .....Psalm 23:4
Confession .....Psalm 51
Consecration .....Philemon 3
Constancy .....Ruth 1
Contrast .....Deuteronomy 28

Converts ..... Psalm 32
Deliverance ..... Acts 12
Divinity ..... John 1
Duty ..... Romans 12
Faith ..... Hebrews 11
Flood ..... Genesis 7
Friendship ..... 1 Samuel 20
Fruit ..... John 15
Gifts ..... 1 Corinthians 12, Luke 3
Gideon's Band ..... Judges 7
Good Shepherd; Service ..... Luke 10, John 10
Heaven ..... John 14
Holy Spirit ..... John 14,15
Humility ..... John 13
Instruction ..... Proverbs 1
Intercession ..... John 17
Jubilee ..... Leviticus 25
Judgment ..... Matthew 25
Law ..... Exodus 20
Life, Frailty of ..... Psalm 90
Love ..... 1 Corinthians 13
Messianic ..... Isaiah 53
Minister's ..... 1 Corinthians 4
Missions ..... Psalm 72;
New Covenant ..... Hebrews 8
Old Age ..... Ecclesiastes 12
Omniscience ..... Psalm 139
Overcomers ..... Revelation 2, 3
Passover ..... Exodus 12
Praise ..... Psalm 103
Prayer ..... Daniel 6; Luke 11, 18
Prosperity ..... Psalm 73

Providence .....Psalm 121
Refuge.....Numbers 35
Regeneration .....John 3
Rest .....Hebrews 4
Resurrection .....1 Corinthians 15
Revival.....2 Chronicles 30
Safety .....Psalm 91
Shepherd .....John 10
Soldier's .....Ephesians 6, Revelation 7, 22
Teacher's.....1 Corinthians 2
Temperance .....Proverbs 23
Tither's .....Malachi 3
Tongue .....James 3
Transfiguration, Joy .....Isaiah 12, Matthew 17
Unity .....Ephesians 4
Vanity .....Ecclesiastes 2
Watchman's .....Ezekiel 33
Water of Life .....John 4
Wisdom .....Proverbs 3
Woman's.....Proverbs 31
Word of God .....Deuteronomy 6
Worship .....Psalm 84, Romans 10

5. VERSES

Old Testament .....23,145 verses
New Testament .....7,957 verses
Middle verse of the Bible .....Psalm 118:8
Middle verse of the Old Testament ...2 Chronicles 20:17
Middle verse of the New Testament .....Acts 17:17

Shortest verse of the Old Testament ..... 1 Chronicles 1:25
Shortest verse of the New Testament ..... John 11:35
Longest verse in the Bible..... Esther 8:9
Verse containing all letters of the alphabet except J: ..... Ezra 7:21
Verse containing all letters of the alphabet except Q and M: ..... Daniel 4:37
Verses alike: ..... Psalm 107:8, 15, 21, 31

6. WORDS

In the Old Testament ..... c. 592,601 words
In the New Testament ..... c. 178,282 words

Special Words in the Bible

Longest word in the Bible is: Maher-shalal-hash-baz (18 letters) ..... Isaiah 8:1

Words Occurring Only Once in the Bible

Advocate..... 1 John 2:1
Chair ..... 2 Kings 4:10
Fervor ..... Zechariah 8:2
Gnat ..... Matthew 23:24

"And" occurs 38,800 times in the Bible.

Father, Father's, Fathers, Fathers' occur in the Bible 1,645 times

Mother, Mothers, Mother's, Mothers' occur 321 times

Boy and boys occur 11 times

Girl and girls occur 26 times

God occurs 4,393 times

Lord occurs 7,766 times

7. LETTERS

In Old Testament ..... c. 2,546,906
In New Testament ..... c. 774,730

8. UNUSUAL THINGS IN THE BIBLE

1. Man who lived to be 969 years old .....Genesis 5:27
2. Sons of God married the daughters of men .....Genesis 6:2
3. Man used a stone for a pillow .....Genesis 28:11
4. Baby had a scarlet thread tied around its hand before it was born .....Genesis 38:28–29
5. Battle won because man stretched out his hand .....Exodus 17:11
6. Man was spoken to by an ass .....Numbers 22:28–30
7. One who had a bed 13½ feet long and 6 feet wide ...Deuteronomy 3:11
8. The women who had to shave their heads before they could marry .....Deuteronomy 21:11–13
9. Women forbidden to wear men's clothing .....Deuteronomy 22:5
10. Sun stood still for a whole day .....Joshua 10:13
11. A woman killed a man by driving a nail through his head.....Judges 4:17–21
12. Men lapped water like dogs.....Judges 7:5
13. An army with seven hundred left-handed men .....Judges 20:16

14. Man whose hair weighed about 6⅔ lb. when it was cut annually .....2 Samuel 14:26
15. Where a ferry boat used ...2 Samuel 19:18
16. Man who had twelve fingers and twelve toes .....2 Samuel 21:20
17. The ax that floated in the water .....2 Kings 6:1–6
18. Woman boiled and ate her son .....2 Kings 6:29
19. Man had seven hundred wives and three hundred concubines .....1 Kings 11:3
20. Father who had eighty-eight children .....2 Chronicles 11:21
21. No taste in the white of an egg .....Job 6:6
22. The sun travelled backward.....Isaiah 38:8
23. Man walked naked for three years.....Isaiah 20:2–3
24. Army of 185,000 destroyed in one night .....Isaiah 37:36
25. A man whose life was increased by 15 years because he prayed .....Isaiah 38:1–5
26. The Bible that was cut with a pen knife .....Jeremiah 36:20–23
27. Graveyard full of dead bones resurrected .....Ezekiel 37
28. A harlot an ancestor of Christ .....Matthew 1:5
29. Man ate locusts for food ...Matthew 3:4

Worship

FILL IN THE BLANKS

1. The earliest musical activity of the Christian Church was _____ _____.

2. "Praise God from whom all _____ flow. Praise him all _____ here below. Praise him _____ ye heavenly hosts. Praise _____, _____, and Holy _____."

3. The Lesser Doxology is also known as the _____ _____.

4. The Greater Doxology is also known as the _____ _____ _____.

ANSWERS p. 400

WORD BANK

singing blessings creatures
Gloria hymn Son
Ghost Patri
Excelsis Gloria in Father
above all

MULTIPLE CHOICE

1. **Dr. Babcock, who wrote the hymn, "This is my Father's World," saw nature as:**
   A. the eagle's natural habitat
   B. the music of the spheres
   C. worthy of worship
   D. a mighty warrior

2. **The hymn, "Beneath the Cross of Jesus" was written by which woman?**
   A. Elizabeth Elliot
   B. Mother Teresa
   C. Elizabeth C. Clephane
   D. Fanny J. Crosby

3. **John Bowring, the author of the hymn, "In the Cross of Christ I Glory," could speak how many languages before he died?**
   A. 3
   B. 20
   C. over 100
   D. 33

4. **The hymn, "There is a Fountain" by William Cowper is based upon what Old Testament text?**
   A. Zechariah 13:1
   B. Psalm 1:3
   C. Genesis 8:2
   D. Job 22:12

5. **"There is a Fountain" was originally titled:**
   - **A.** Let the River Flow
   - **B.** Peace for the Fountain Opened
   - **C.** Love love me do
   - **D.** Many waters

HOW ABOUT THAT!

Contrary to popular opinion, *Away in a Manger,* was not written by Martin Luther—in fact, it's almost unknown in Germany!

6. **The writer of "Be Thou My Vision" was what nationality?**
   - **A.** Irish
   - **B.** Yiddish
   - **C.** Scottish
   - **D.** Hungarian

ANSWERS p. 400

7. **"Jesus, I My Cross Have Taken" was written in which century?**
   - **A.** 8th
   - **B.** 20th
   - **C.** 19th
   - **D.** 17th

8. "The King of Love My Shepherd is" is based on what scripture?

A. Psalm 119
B. Psalm 23
C. Psalm 69
D. Psalm 73

MATCHING

1. O Love that Wilt Not Let Me Go	a. Charles Wesley
2. I Surrender All	b. Isaac Watts
3. Joy to the World	c. Elizabeth P. Prentiss
4. The Church's One Foundation	d. Henry F. Lyte
5. More Love to Thee	e. Jean Sophia Pigott
6. Jesus, I am Resting, Resting	f. Joseph Addison
7. Hark! the Herald Angels Sing	g. George Matheson
8. When All Thy Mercies, O My God	h. Samuel J. Stone
9. Take My Life and Let It Be	i. Judson W. Van De Venter
10. Jesus, I My Cross Have Taken	j. Frances R. Havergal

FILL IN THE BLANKS

Gregorian Chant

1. Gregorian chant was invented _____ a system of _____ writing had been invented.

2. Gregorian chant was invented because Charlemagne, king of the _____, wanted music in his kingdom to be sung like in _____.

3. Gregorian chant was named after a _____ of that period in order to give it greater _____.

4. _____ monks, in the _____ century, restored the melodies of the chants to their pre-seventeenth century forms.

ANSWERS p. 401

WORD BANK

Solesmes Gregorian nineteenth
eighteenth king music after
before Franks Rome authority
English pope

UNSCRAMBLE

1. Rome Vole ot Hete
2. Kaet Ym Eilf dan Elt ti Eb
3. Ganizam Ercag
4. Nitles Hingt
5. No Ronjads Roymst Skanb
6. Hertwi Anth Owns
7. Anthebe het Sorcs fo Sujes
8. Wrodan Tinahrics Resilosd
9. Yaaw ni a Gernam
10. Lelhalhaju, Thaw a Virsoa

FILL IN THE BLANKS

How Well Do You Know the Hymns?

1. _____ grace, how sweet the _____
   That saved a _____ like me!
   I _____ was lost, but now am found.
   Was _____ but now I _____!

When we've been _____ ten thousand years,

_____ shining as the _____,

We've ____ less days to _____ _____'s _____.

Than when we've first _____.

ANSWERS p. 402

2. _____ as I am, without one _____

But that thy _____ was shed for me

And that thou _____ me come to thee

O Lamb of God, ____ _____! ____ _____!

Just as I am, thy _____ unknown

Hath broken every _____ down

Now to be _____, yea _____ alone

O Lamb of God, ____ _____! ____ _____!

3. O for a thousand _____ to sing

My great Redeemer's _____

The _____ of my God and King

The _____ of his grace.

_____ him ye _____, his praise ye dumb

Your loosened tongues _____

Ye blind behold your Savior _____

And _____ ye lame for joy.

TRUE OR FALSE

1. The word worship is used 223 times in the Bible.

2. "Worship" comes from Hebrew and Greek words that mean "Bow Down."

3. The hymn of worship that Mary sings in the New Testament when she discovers that she will bear the child Jesus is called *The Holy Confession.*

4. Worship in the Old Testament included making sacrifices.

5. David built the first Temple in which the Israelites worshiped God.

6. A worship service in the Old Testament Tabernacle included a person confessing their sins, making a sacrifice, sprinkling blood on the altar, the priest pronouncing them forgiven.

7. Worship in the New Testament synagogue consisted of lessons, singing, eating, sermons, and prayers.

8. All hymns are males.

9. In the synagogue, the Torah was chanted from beginning to end every year.

10. Liturgies of the Christian church vary according to the country in which they are read.

WORD SEARCH

(up and down, backwords, diagonal—any which way)

ANSWERS p. 404

Amazing Grace
Blessed Assurance
Just As I Am
Rugged Cross
Jesus Loves Me
Holy Holy Holy
Amazing Love

P	J	V	R	I	B	C	D	S	G	K	O	T	Y	R	E	H	K	V	C
A	M	A	Z	I	N	G	G	R	A	C	E	Z	W	R	J	L	O	S	G
M	N	V	D	X	J	H	R	I	P	E	D	J	L	A	I	R	H	K	O
U	F	H	M	V	X	D	H	K	P	C	J	M	H	F	S	E	Y	I	N
L	N	V	R	H	R	F	J	L	P	W	O	E	V	M	J	F	J	L	T
M	E	R	A	O	O	V	C	S	E	V	O	L	G	N	I	Z	A	M	A
L	G	U	A	B	U	L	K	B	D	G	K	L	P	H	C	D	W	F	K
B	Y	G	A	G	K	O	Y	N	F	S	C	J	O	U	R	S	V	N	K
L	V	G	B	C	G	K	I	H	D	B	M	K	H	F	B	K	L	F	S
V	H	E	J	F	G	K	L	H	O	G	D	H	L	O	G	E	U	P	P
B	S	D	H	D	J	E	S	U	S	L	O	V	E	S	M	E	J	D	S
K	F	C	C	H	K	P	G	F	J	P	Y	V	D	H	L	V	S	Y	O
M	O	R	E	F	N	D	H	K	F	D	K	H	G	D	X	N	K	F	S
M	G	O	N	F	S	H	K	E	N	C	A	T	O	J	C	Z	X	H	S
N	D	S	V	G	K	F	S	G	K	L	B	B	D	L	B	D	F	J	K
M	F	S	N	F	D	N	K	H	S	M	V	D	G	M	Y	M	V	D	J
N	C	C	H	H	F	C	N	K	F	D	K	G	D	H	K	G	X	N	I
N	F	S	J	K	G	C	I	N	G	D	M	A	I	S	A	T	S	U	J
B	D	D	J	G	D	T	K	V	E	G	J	F	D	H	J	F	D	V	A
B	L	E	S	S	E	D	A	S	S	U	R	A	N	C	E	H	N	F	F

PUT THE FOLLOWING IN ORDER

(when these hymns were written, from oldest to most recent)

Because He Lives

Be Thou My Vision

He Lives

O Perfect Love

O Sacred Head, Now Wounded

The Solid Rock

Tis So Sweet to Trust in Jesus

ANSWERS p. 405

Turn Your Eyes Upon Jesus

Joy to the World

I Need Thee Every Hour

FILL IN THE BLANKS

Christmas Carols!

1. Silent night, _____ night!

   All is calm, all is _____.

   Round _____ Virgin, Mother and Child.

   Holy _____ so tender and mild,

   Sleep in heavenly peace,

   Sleep in heavenly peace.

   Silent night, holy night!

   _____ quake at the sight.

   _____ stream from heaven afar

   Heavenly hosts sing _____,

   Christ the Savior is born!

   Christ the Savior is born.

   Silent night, holy night!

   _____ love's pure light.

   _____ beams from Thy holy face

ANSWERS p. 405

With dawn of _____ grace,

Jesus Lord, at Thy birth.

Jesus Lord, at Thy birth.

2. O _____, all ye faithful,

Joyful and _____,

O come ye, O come ye to _____;

Come and _____ Him,

Born the King of _____;

O come, let us adore Him,

O come, let us adore Him,

O come, let us adore Him,

Christ, the Lord.

Sing, _____ of angels,

Sing in _____,

O sing all ye _____ of heaven above;

Glory to God,

All glory in the highest;

Yea, Lord we _____ thee,

Born this _____ morning,

Jesus, to thee be all _____ given;

_____ of the Father,

Now in flesh appearing;

3. O holy night! The _____ are brightly shining

It is the _____ of the dear Savior's birth!

_____ lay the world in sin and error pining

Till he appear'd and the soul felt its _____.

A _____ of hope the weary world rejoices

For _____ breaks a new and glorious morn!

Fall on your _____

Oh hear the _____ voices

Oh night _____

Oh night when Christ was born

Oh night divine

Oh night divine

Led by the light of Faith _____ beaming
With _____ hearts by His cradle we stand
So led by light of a _____ sweetly gleaming
Here come the wise men from _____ land
The King of Kings lay _____ in lowly manger
In all our _____ born to be our friend

_____ He taught us to love one another
His _____ is love and His gospel is peace
_____ shall He break for the slave is our brother
And in His name all _____ shall cease
Sweet _____ of joy in grateful chorus raise we,
Let all within us _____ His holy name.

4. Bring a torch, _____, Isabella
Bring a torch, to the _____ run!
It is Jesus good _____ of the village;
Christ is born and _____ calling;
Ah! ah! _____ is the mother
Ah! ah! beautiful is her _____!

It is wrong when the _____ is sleeping
It is wrong to _____ so loud;
Silence, all, as you gather around.
Lest your noise should waken Jesus.
Hush! hush! see how _____ he sleeps!

Top Ten Rejected Christmas Carols

10. We Wish You a Hairy Christmas

9. Got Arrested, You Merry Gentlemen?

8. Hark, Harold the Angel Sneezes!

7. I Saw Three Ships Sink

6. I Might Be Home for Christmas

5. Santa Claus Is Coming to Get Me

4. The Day After Christmas

3. Rudolph, the Red-nosed Chandelier

2. We Three Kings Disoriented Are

1. O Come All Ye Hangnails!

Hasten now, good _____ of the village;
Hasten now the Christ Child to _____.
You will find him _____ in the manger;
_____ come and whisper softly,
Hush! hush! _____ now he sleeps.

Softly to the little _____.
Softly in a _____ come;
Look and see how _____ is Jesus
how he is white, his cheeks are _____!
Hush! hush! see how the _____ is sleeping;
Hush! hush! see how he _____ in his dreams.

HOW ABOUT THAT!

The tune to *A Mighty Fortress* was taken from a popular bar song during Martin Luther's life.

5. Good Christian men, _____
With heart and _____ and voice;
Give ye _____ to what we say;
News! News! Jesus _____ is born today!

_____ and ass before him bow, he is in the manger now;

Christ is born today! Christ is born today!

Good _____ men, rejoice,

With _____ and soul and voice;

Now ye hear of endless _____,

Jesus Christ was _____ for this!

He has _____ the heav'nly door

And man is blessed evermore.

Christ was born for _____! Christ was born for _____!

_____ Christian men, rejoice,

With heart and soul and _____;

Now ye _____ not fear the grave;

Jesus Christ is born to _____.

_____ you one and calls you all,

To gain His everlasting _____.

Christ was born to save! Christ was born to save!

If you want to know when Charles Wesley wrote his first song, you'll have to ask hymn!

ANSWERS TO: WORSHIP

FILL IN THE BLANKS

#	ANSWER
1.	hymn singing
2.	blessings, creatures, above, Father, Son, Ghost
3.	Gloria Patri
4.	Gloria in Excelsis

MULTIPLE CHOICE

#	ANSWER
1.	b
2.	c
3.	c
4.	a
5.	b
6.	a
7.	c
8.	b

MATCHING

#	ANSWER
1.	g
2.	i
3.	b
4.	h
5.	c
6.	e
7.	a
8.	f
9.	j
10.	d

FILL IN THE BLANKS

#	ANSWER
1.	before, music
2.	Franks, Rome
3.	Pope, authority
4.	Solesmes, nineteenth

UNSCRAMBLE

#	ANSWER
1.	More Love to Thee
2.	Take My Life and Let It Be

UNSCRAMBLE—cont'd

#	ANSWER
3.	Amazing Grace
4.	Silent Night
5.	On Jordan's Stormy Banks
6.	Whiter Than Snow
7.	Beneath the Cross of Jesus
8.	Onward, Christian Soldiers
9.	Away in a Manger
10.	Hallelujah, What a Savior

FILL IN THE BLANKS

#	ANSWER
1.	Amazing, sound wretch once blind, see there bright, sun no, sing, God, praise begun
2.	Just, plea blood bidst I come, I come

#	ANSWER
	love
	barrier
	thine, thine
	I come, I come
3.	tongues
	praise
	glories
	triumphs
	hear, deaf
	employ
	come
	leap

TRUE OR FALSE

#	ANSWER	REFERENCE
1.	False	each translation is different
2.	True	
3.	False	*Magnificat*
4.	True	
5.	False	Solomon built the Temple
6.	True	
7.	False	no eating
8.	False!	
9.	True	
10.	True	

WORD SEARCH

P J V R I B C D S G K O T Y R E H K V C
A M A Z I N G G R A C E Z W R J L O S G
M N V D X J H R I P E D J L A I R H K O
U F H M V X D H K P C J M H F S E Y I N
L N V R H R F J L P W O E V M J F J L T
M E R A O O V C S E V O L G N I Z A M A
L G U A B U L K B D G K L P H C D W F K
B Y G A G K O Y N F S C J O U R S V N K
L V G B C G K I H D B M K H F B K L F S
V H E J F G K L H O G D H L O G E U P P
B S D H D J E S U S L O V E S M E J D S
K F C C H K P G F J P Y V D H L V S Y O
M O R E F N D H K F D K H G D X N K F S
M G O N F S H K E N C A T O J C Z X H S
N D S V G K F S G K L B B D L B D F J K
M F S N F D N K H S M V D G M Y M V D J
N C C H H F C N K F D K G D H K G X N I
N F S J K G C I N G D M A I S A T S U J
B D D J G D T K V E G J F D H J F D V A
B L E S S E D A S S U R A N C E H N F F

Q. What did the pastor's hands say to his arms?
A. Onward Christian shoulders!

PUT THE FOLLOWING IN ORDER

#	ANSWER	DATE
1.	Be Thou My Vision	8th c.
2.	O Sacred Head, Now Wounded	12th c.
3.	Joy to the World	1719
4.	The Solid Rock	1834
5.	I Need Thee Every Hour	1872
6.	Tis So Sweet to Trust in Jesus	1879
7.	O Perfect Love	1883
8.	Turn Your Eyes Upon Jesus	1918
9.	He Lives	1933
10.	Because He Lives	1960s

FILL IN THE BLANKS

#	ANSWER
1.	holy, bright, yon, infant shepherds, glories, alleluia Son of God, radiant, redeeming
2.	come, triumphant, Bethlehem, behold, Angels choirs, exultation, citizens greet, happy, glory, Word

FILL IN THE BLANKS—cont'd

#	ANSWER
3.	stars, night, long, worth, thrill, yonder knees, angel, divine serenely, glowing, star, Orient, thus, trials truly, law, chains, oppression, hymns, praise
4.	Jeanette, cradle, folks, Mary beautiful, son, Child, talk fast, folk, see, asleep, quietly, peacefully stable, moment, charming, rosey, child, smiling
5.	rejoice, soul, heed, Christ, ox Christian, heart, bliss, born, op'ed, this, this good, voice, need, save, calls, hall